Young W
POETRY COM

CH00614034

GREAT MINDS

Your World...Your Future...YOUR WORDS

- Inspirations From
The Midlands
Edited by Jessica Woodbridge

 Young**Writers**

First published in Great Britain in 2005 by:
Young Writers
Remus House
Coltsfoot Drive
Peterborough
PE2 9JX
Telephone: 01733 890066
Website: www.youngwriters.co.uk

SB ISBN 1 84602 191 X

Foreword

This year, the Young Writers' 'Great Minds' competition proudly presents a showcase of the best poetic talent selected from over 40,000 up-and-coming writers nationwide.

Young Writers was established in 1991 to promote the reading and writing of poetry within schools and to the youth of today. Our books nurture and inspire confidence in the ability of young writers and provide a snapshot of poems written in schools and at home by budding poets of the future.

The thought, effort, imagination and hard work put into each poem impressed us all and the task of selecting poems was a difficult but nevertheless enjoyable experience.

We hope you are as pleased as we are with the final selection and that you and your family continue to be entertained with *Great Minds - Inspirations From The Midlands* for many years to come.

Contents

Suria Mahmood (13)	46
Fatima Bibi (13)	46
Rukhsahr Iqbal (12)	47
Anisha Ali (13)	47
Halima Ali (13)	48
Rishma Khan (12)	48
Sameena Asghar (13)	48
Aashiya Rahman (12)	49
Henna Parveen (13)	49
Muriam Butt (15)	50

Brownhills High School, Stoke-on-Trent

Nicola Pedley (13)	50
Rachel Forrester (13)	51
Natalie Leese (13)	51
Laura Pointon (13)	52

Cradley High School, Halesowen

Jade Whitehouse (14)	52
Hollie Foster (14)	53
Ashley Edwards (12)	53
Emma Wilkinson (13)	54
Sohaib Qamar (12)	54
Christine Stafford (14)	55
Stefanie Davies (13)	55
Huma Javed (13)	56
Aron Jones (13)	56
Hayley Nock-Radford (12)	57
Katrina Haycock (13)	57
Carmen Phuah (13)	58
Matthew Heathcock (12)	58
Amy Cooper (12)	59
Kirsty Bunn (12)	59
Kelly Billingham (13)	60
Laura Cadman (13)	60
Jade Fowkes (13)	61
Matthew Plant (12)	61
Leanne Morgan (13)	62
Faiza Salim (13)	63
Zak Horan (12)	64
Phillip Cook (12)	64

Leah Jones (13)   65
Michael Hickman (12)   65
Rebecca James (13)   66
Abdulla Salam (12)   66

Dayncourt School Specialist Sports College, Radcliffe-on-Trent

Matthew Jones (11)   67
Katie Fletcher (11)   67
Ria Mills (11)   68
Victoria Coates (12)   68
Chris Marshall (12)   69
Natalie White (12)   69
Emily May Woodhouse (11)   70
Leah Woodford (12)   71
Claire Leivers (12)   72
Jonathan Horn (11)   73
Hanna Hulme (13)   74
Kara Forrest (13)   74
Jack Cox (12)   75
Sarah Gell (13)   75
Elizabeth Winter (12)   76
Rebecca Gill (13)   77
Ryan Geere (12)   77
Aaron Denham (13)   78
Abi Kennie (12)   78
Adele Goodwin (12)   79
Joe Perkins (12)   79
Lauren Stevenson (13)   79
Rachel McDermott (12)   80
Joseph Mascia (11)   80
Evie Stannard (13)   81

Farnborough School Technology College, Nottingham

Chelsea Launder (13)   81
Kayleigh Dickinson (12)   82
Luke Needham (13)   82
David Hopkin (12)   83
Tom Wells (12)   83
Ashley Richardson (13)   84
James Freeman (13)   84
Laura Kirby (12)   85

Kathryn Sargent (13)	85
Karissa Brewster (13)	86
Megan Hobson (12)	86
Alicia Leeanne Hoad (13)	87
Kirstin Rowan (13)	88
Ellie Sewell (12)	89

Henry Mellish Comprehensive School, Nottingham

Reece Hutchinson (11)	89
Shelley Smith (11)	90
Chantelle Watson (11)	90
Nyala Skerritt (13)	90
Levi Pollard (12)	91
Priscilla Chakana (11)	91
Amie Godber (11)	92
Luke Ashcroft (11)	92
Luke Brown (13)	92
Danielle Bowler (12)	93
Sam Butler (11)	93
Chris McGuire (13)	93
Jordan Brandom (13)	94
Katie Bignall (11)	94
Kane McLean (12)	95
Sophie Sanderson (12)	95
Kim Gough (13)	95
Hayleigh Walker-Randle (12)	95
Marie Pearce (12)	96
Victoria Fowler (13)	96
Michael Tyers (13)	96

King Edward VI College, Stourbridge

Benjamin Catt (16)	97
Natasha Hussain (16)	98

Lordswood Girls' School, Birmingham

Aneela Aziz (12)	98
Samiye Mazlum (11)	99
Rosie Stokes-Chaplin (11)	99
Samera Shane (15)	100
Sabrina Samra (12)	100

Jessica Barnett (13)	139
Joe Wilkinson (11)	139
Shannon Gilmore (12)	140
Chris Page (14)	141
Kalie-Dee Jones (12)	142
Amie Murphy (11)	142
Liam Revell (14)	143
Fallon Leigh Done (11)	143
Mark Sierotko (11)	144
Louise Farrell (12)	144
Faye Allison (12)	145
Hannah Jackson (12)	145
Megan Fussell (13)	146
Caitlin Curtis (12)	147
Aisling Hanna (13)	148
Venetia Wright (11)	148
Sarah Wilson (12)	149
Charlotte Pearson (11)	149
Maria Birnie (12)	150
Joan Carr (15)	151
Eilish O'Loghlen (11)	152
David Birch (12)	152
Thomas Rogers (16)	153
Emil Tangham (11)	153

Shepshed High School, Loughborough

Jo Nash (14)	154
Philip Bell-Young (13)	155

Stafford Grammar School, Stafford

Elizabeth Egan (12)	156
Tom Harris (14)	156
Callum Beddoes (12)	157
Joanna Craig (12)	157
Samuel White (11)	158
Tim Hawkins (14)	158
Rebekah Martin (11)	159
Ashleigh Eden (13)	160
Joshua Groom (11)	161
Adam Cotton (13)	161
William Housden (13)	162

Alex Roberts (14)	192
David Fallah (12)	193
George Mason (12)	194
Emma Bailey (13)	194
Paul Greaves (14)	195
Joshua Chick (14)	195
Dominic Moseley (11)	196
Ian Watt (14)	197
Jack Atkinson-Willes (11)	198
Ruth Millington (13)	198
Philip Spragg (12)	199
Michael Yates (15)	199
Ben Hughes (14)	200
Hannah Inglis (12)	201
Ginny Tallent (13)	202
Nicholas Lawrence (14)	203
Sophie Bohanan (13)	204
Jacob Billington (11)	205
Sam Shaw (14)	206
James Yeo (12)	206
Rebecca Hawkins (11)	207
William Stuart (14)	207
Nick Bourne (11)	208
Srinivas Cheruvu (13)	209
Jessica Keitley (14)	210
Nicholas Henderson (15)	211

The Grange School, Stourbridge

Shane Cox (13)	211
Chloe Salter (13)	212
Ami Bevan (13)	212
Jordanna Holton (13)	213
Katie Middleton (13)	213
Tracey Evans (13)	214
Kyomi Johnson (13)	214
Christopher Perks (12)	215
Sam Capewell (12)	215
David Tibbetts (12)	215
Leigh Dooner (13)	216
Alice Barker (12)	216
Rhiannon Leonard (13)	217

Robyn Goodfellow (12)	235
Hayley Chatfield (12)	236
Alex Shaw (11)	237
Sarah Daniels (12)	237
Amy Courtney (12)	237
Jim Mulherin (12)	238
Jasmin Hellard (12)	238
Emma Child (11)	239
Lucy Thompson (11)	239
Hannah Fyfe (12)	240
Mike Green (11)	240
Amy-May Boyce (12)	241
Katrina Tompkins (11)	241
Mikey Pointon (11)	242
Sam Coates (12)	242
Megan Hitchin (12)	242
Lucinda Grinsted (11)	243
Ben Thompson (11)	243
Holly Corfield-Carr (17)	244
Jack Cuthbert (12)	245

Wigmore High School, Wigmore

Brad Giffard (13)	245

Windsor Park CE Middle School, Uttoxeter

Laura Bradley-Smith (13)	246
Jennifer Lee-Bromley (13)	247
David Harris (12)	248
Sarah Lomas (12)	249
Georgette Storey (13)	250
Michael Gascoigne (13)	251
Lauren Swinson (13)	252
Lydia Nadine (12)	253
Stephanie Gear (12)	254

The Poems

War

Rockets come flying,
The people are dying,
Women are running,
Their children are crying.

Tanks are thundering down the streets,
Past the dead all wrapped in sheets.
Soldiers positioned in their turrets
Keeping a look out for enemy bullets.

Somebody's son, somebody's brother,
Keeping an eye on each other.
They're loyal and true and work as a team
As they all keep watch for the enemy unseen.

Another country, another war
More misery to endure.
When will all the fighting cease
So all the world can live in peace?

Dan Plant (14)
Alleyne's High School, Stone

Jack Frost!

Jack Frost was as cold as ice,
But then he still needed to sacrifice,
As I entered the frost, shrivelled and cold,
My eyes would water and then go bold.

My feet would freeze,
Like a cold breeze,
This is Jack Frost who's playing around,
Like a tiger prowling proud.

Jack Frost is the sound of an enormous slush,
Although he is a mighty big push,
My friend Jack Frost,
Who is never ever lost.

Danielle Chadwick
Alleyne's High School, Stone

If Only Life Was Longer

Outside the window the world was clotted with trees,
As more and more cars sped by.
The moon shone down on the darkened motorway,
As my mum's eyes flickered when she drove.
At this point I knew she was tired,
She closed her eyes to go to sleep,
The car swerved off the moonlit road,
We passed many different trees
And straight into the ocean-like lake.
We sunk as I saw fish through my window,
Water started to find its way in.
I was scared, really scared, too scared,
I held my breath as the water flooded the car,
At that very point I knew that this was it,
Flashbacks filled my mind to haunt me,
I regretted everything bad I had ever done,
I knew this was meant to happen,
If only life was longer,
I could have changed.

Simon Humphries (14)
Alleyne's High School, Stone

My Dog Frazer

My dog's coat is ruby red,
Like a chestnut the owner said,
My dog is happy and cheerful,
He isn't ever sad or tearful.
His eyes glare like a hawk,
He refuses to eat with a knife and fork.
His coat is beautiful and shines like the sun.
As he wakes in the morning,
His main priority is to have some fun.

His name is *Frazer* and we love him so,
We dread the time he may have to go.

Daniel Humphries (14)
Alleyne's High School, Stone

Wine Is The Drink

Wine is the drink made from the vine
Wine is the drink of pleasure divine

Wine is the drink of kings
Wine is the drink that makes us sing

Wine is the drink of love
Wine is the drink that is as smooth as a dove

Wine is the drink that comes from France
Wine is the drink that makes you dance

Wine is the drink that my dad drinks
Wine is the drink that makes us think

Wine is the drink that comes in barrels
Wine is the drink we drink after carols

Wine is the drink that is put on posters
Wine is the drink that causes boasters!

Wine is the drink we see in books
Wine is a drink with different looks

Wine is a drink that you have in church
Wine is a drink that helps you search

Wine is a drink made from the vine
Wine is a drink of pleasure divine.

Joshua Wilson
Alleyne's High School, Stone

Untitled

Christmas is full of life
Not like the turkey
Everyone opening gifts
Eating, drinking, laughing
Snow falls on the ground
Silently
Everyone is having fun.

Taya Millman
Alleyne's High School, Stone

Fear

Fear is waiting in the queue for a roller coaster ride.
Fear is the dark from which you try to hide.
Fear is knowing there is nowhere else to go.
Fear is the voice, of which the owls throw.
Fear is the dark on a cold stormy night.
Fear is the horror, the thriller and the fright.
Fear is like the bat in the night
Screeching and swooping from left to right.
Fear is knowing what comes next.
Fear is the witch's evil hex.
You can't hide from fear, neither can you run.
You can't hear fear, you can't see it come.
Fear will find everyone for one second or one day.
You can try to hide from fear, but you can't get away.
You can run for the rest of your days.
Fear is an axe that gently sways.

Sam Doyle
Alleyne's High School, Stone

My Paper Round

It's time for my paper round
The rain lashes on the waterlogged ground
Sheets of rain
Overflowing drains
Riverbanks burst
Making floods worse
Car splashes by
The water rises high
Like a tidal wave
I'm nearly in an early grave
Paper bag as heavy as lead
As pools of water wash over my head
Clothes cling like a second skin
Run me a hot bath so I can hop in.

Jack Edmunds
Alleyne's High School, Stone

Fear

Fear is dark
Fear is horror
Fear is cold but yet so bold
Fear is death
Fear is life
Fear is like a bloodbath fight
Fear is monsters
Fear is ghosts
Fear is the enemy that tortures the most
Fear is fast
Fear is slow
Fear is the frost when it hits your toe
Fear is sadness
Fear is tears
Fear is the bullet when it hits your ears
Fear is bad
Fear is mad
Fear is the day when your whole family is sad.

Joe Fares
Alleyne's High School, Stone

Weather

Wind is like a speeding train
Charging down the track
Sending you back with every blow

Rain can make you go all wet
Like you have just had a shower
Sending you back in all misery

Hail can make you shout out in pain
Like you have just been kicked
Also sending you back in misery

The sun is like a god
Letting you play out
Making you sweat like a tired runner.

Thomas Breeze (13)
Alleyne's High School, Stone

Gift Or Goal

I'm only young and have no goals,
But goals are all I seek,
In school I felt a normal child
And never reached my peak.
Sports I thought and so I tried,
But my time was taken up,
What kind of 'thing' was left to try,
That was easy to pick up.

In all I tried I *did* succeed,
But none were ever right
And one more thing came to mind,
I'd keep it with me *tight*.
This idea was the best so far,
But still to put to practice,
The thing that had run in my family for so long,
Was nothing as simple as a *kiss*.

At last it found me, my silver and gold,
A talent a gift I'd finally been crowned,
I'm only young and have no goals
And goals are all I found.

Dean Oliver
Alleyne's High School, Stone

The Seaside

The beach in winter so quiet and deserted,
The waves crash on the rocks,
The icy water like frost on a winter's morning.
The beach in summer so colourful and busy,
Sandcastles, rock pools and ice cream,
The sea alive with the sound of laughter.

Robert Jolliffe
Alleyne's High School, Stone

We Like To Think

The clouds are as light as a feather
The clouds are as white as paper
The clouds are as fluffy as sheep
The clouds are my sweet dream

The grass is green as a unripe banana
The grass is as thin as a piece of thread
The grass is as short as a hair on a man's face
The grass is a whole field of fun

The sea is as blue as a bird
The sea is as smooth as a newborn baby
The sea is as cold as a block of ice
The sea is the ocean world.

Jessica Lytollis (14)
Alleyne's High School, Stone

Loving?

Loving is the thing you like the best,
Loving is liking but is to like to love?

Hating is the thing that seals your fears
Hating is the things that steals your tears.

Living is the thing that inspires you the most,
Living is seeing, laughing and crying, not to boast.

Fearing is the thing that prowls in the dark,
Fearing is the teeth of the dangerous shark.

Smiling is the warmth in the ones we befriend,
Smiling is the realisation of sadness at the end.

Loving is the thing you like the best,
Loving is liking but is to like to love?

Bethanie Shingler
Alleyne's High School, Stone

Poem About Christmas

C hristmas is a happy time of joy
H oliday time and lots of toys
R ejoicing and merry
I nvite the family for a glass of sherry
S nowy weather is cold and white
T obogganing all day and night
M erry Christmas each and everyone
A nd happy new year, hope you have fun
S ing, eat, drink and be merry.

Lauren Redshaw
Alleyne's High School, Stone

Netball Tournament Ballad

Ball flying down the court
Hands ready to catch,
It's a well known fact
We were gonna win the match.

It was then half-time
We were getting excited,
We had a chance of winning this
And Miss Gill was delighted!

We were into our last game,
We were almost there,
Just one more goal to go,
Or we would all despair!

It was down to the last minute,
We would have had our chance,
But we lost it fair and square
And came third place and danced!

Rhianne Lilley (13)
Baverstock Specialist Sports College And Foundation School, Druids Heath

Football Fantasy

It was coming up to ten past six,
And as I passed the crisps to Dean,
The excitement grew inside ourselves,
With our eyes glued on the screen.

It was the World Cup final of 2006,
The teams were England and Brazil,
I was surprised that we had got this far,
But the score was still nil nil.

My eyes got as heavy as a steamroller,
They couldn't help but close,
Until a familiar voice said to me,
'C'mon lads, on yer toes.'

I looked up to see the England coach,
Who, in my eyes, was the devil,
'Listen, quick,' he said to me,
'Always pass to Neville.'

They paused the game to substitute,
And off came Kieran Dyer,
I took his place in right midfield,
In the crowd was Lizzie Maguire.

Shortly after, it was a corner to us,
Which was taken by Paul Scholes,
Who crossed the ball in and it hit off the bar,
So I ran in and scored a goal!

The crowd went mental with excitement,
I turned round and started to run,
The scene went dark and a familiar voice said,
'Wake up, mate. England have won!'

Jake Harborne (12)
Baverstock Specialist Sports College And Foundation School, Druids Heath

My Brother

My brother joined the army,
A couple of years ago.
We weren't allowed to contact him,
So my mother, she felt really low.

He went through lots of training
And was thrown up the wall
And when he was good he got a reward,
Like playing a game of football.

He stayed there for a long time,
He made lots of friends.
With his Corporal, Sweetman, Tez,
Their friendship never ends.

My brother then met the Queen,
No it's not a lie.
But imagine how embarrassed he was,
When my mum started to cry.

And then we went to watch him,
Getting his first gun.
It looked as though his army life
Had really just begun.

He left the army after a couple of years,
Say it isn't so.
He stayed at home most of the time
And our friendship began to grow.

Hayley Ensor (12)
Baverstock Specialist Sports College And Foundation School, Druids Heath

Tsunami Ballad

We sat at home,
That Boxing Day,
Dwelling upon our last Christmas gifts,
When it took lives away.

Towering over frightened tourists,
Its icy breath drew you in,
Rising, rising higher and higher still,
Flooding round you, drenching your skin.

Screeching,shouting all around,
Buildings bashed, viciously wrecked,
Cars toppled by the almighty wave,
On the landscape a fearful effect.

The wave goes in and retreats,
Causing suffering and heartache,
Families torn from one another,
Mother Nature has made a great mistake.

Finally it leaves, leaving anguish,
Time to pull together as one,
They need all the help they can get,
Let's work together to see what can be done.

Countries heard and decided to help,
Sending supplies that are necessary,
All the nations united,
As there are many bodies to bury.

Rebecca Walker (12)
Baverstock Specialist Sports College And Foundation School, Druids Heath

Double Death Ballad

There was a terror on this night
But no one knew but them
Everyone was fast asleep
This was all after ten

The people were mean and keen
The first was dirty Den
The next was mean as most, Andy
No they're not gentlemen

One isn't dead, yet soon will be
One was pushed off a bridge
Den finally killed by Chrissy
Then landed on a ridge

There were two tragedies that night
No one really cared
They might come and get them next week
Everyone was scared.

Carl Oliver (12)
Baverstock Specialist Sports College And Foundation School, Druids Heath

Bugsy Malone Performance Ballad

Getting ready for the big night,
Costumes on the floor,
We're all really excited,
As the audience comes through the door.

Girls add touches to their make-up,
The boys put on their hats,
We're all taking photos
And having loads of laughs.

'He's a sinner, candy coated,'
Adam Tomes starts to sing,
The dressing room is full of nerves,
Worried about everything!

We started to walk on the stage,
The band began to play,
Me, Rhianne and Lisa,
Performed the night away.

Sara Exall (12)
Baverstock Specialist Sports College And Foundation School, Druids Heath

Morning On A Pirate Ship

'Heave ho, me hearties,' said Cut-throat Pete
As he rubbed his eyes and got to his feet,
'It's Tuesday today we've raiding to do.'
Schooners and merchant men out on the blue
Black Bob the cook still lay in his bed
So Pete took his cutlass
And cut through the thread of his hammock
Bob fell on the floor
Pete shouted, 'Get cooking,' as he stormed through the door

Up on the deck the crew were all busy
Scrubbing the boards
Hoisting the sails
And rolling the kegs of gunpowder
Should gunfire fail.

The bells were rung and breakfast was served
They took their seats and were about to eat
When the captain yelled, 'Attack!'
They took their positions and looked for the villains
While Pete fed his bacon to the cat.

For Bob was the worst cook you have ever seen
He was no disciple to nouvelle cuisine.

Hannah Twiname (12)
Baverstock Specialist Sports College And Foundation School, Druids Heath

Homework

Homework is awful,
It should be made unlawful.
Maths makes me flap,
I feel like I'm in a trap.
English is boring,
You'll find me snoring.
Science makes me weep,
Then you'll find me asleep.
RE is a pain,
It should be run over by a train.
PE makes me sweat,
And it also makes me fret!
They make me go swimming,
But I know I'm not winning.
IT is just great,
A subject I don't hate.
Then there's history,
That's just a mystery.
Geography should never have been invented,
The person must've been demented.
Then there's DT and art,
They make me smart!

Amar Kundhi (12)
Baverstock Specialist Sports College And Foundation School, Druids Heath

To My Monkey

When I saw you in the zoo
I couldn't help but like you
When you swung in your cage
When you went out in a rage
I couldn't help but like you.

When you ate your food
When you got in a mood
When you munched on bananas
Singing, 'Oh ah ah ha ha,'
I couldn't help but like you.

When you went away
That ruined my day
You were my monkey
And I like you so much
Saw you eating bananas and such.

Oh monkey
I really liked you
Screeched and moaned
I huffed and puffed and groaned
I wanted my monkey back.

When I saw you again
My heart was not the same
I'm glad that you're back
I like you monkey.

Owen Claridge (12)
Baverstock Specialist Sports College And Foundation School, Druids Heath

My Hamster

My hamster's name is Hattie,
She scampers all around,
But when she's hanging from her cage,
Her feet don't touch the ground.

The other day she gave me,
Such an awful fright,
She escaped from the cage,
In the middle of the night.

The colour of her fur is grey,
Therefore she's pretty hard to find,
All the places she could be,
Began to cross my mind.

Guess where I found her?
Asleep in my bed,
As I went to go to sleep,
She crawled onto my head.

It was lucky I found her,
And she hadn't been lost,
That would have been my pocket money,
To cover how much she cost.

The favourite thing she likes to do,
Is spin in her wheel,
Followed by a short nap,
Then a munch on apple peel.

That's my little hamster,
Hattie is her name,
As cunning as she is,
Escaping is her game.

Nicola Attenborrow (12)
Baverstock Specialist Sports College And Foundation School, Druids Heath

Tony Blair

His name is Blair, but no one knows
The reasons behind his ideas,
He meets the people and greets them well
But fails to see their fears.

He travels the world with his chauffeur
And acts like he is the best.
Starts debates, rows and even wars,
Then leaves it up to the rest.

He meets the Queen who says, 'Hello,
How are you keeping Mr Blair?'
But the troubles are about to start,
As Britain's temper's about to flare.

He lives at 10 Downing Street
And his wife Cherie helps him out,
But time is short for Mr Blair
As the British want him out.

Emily Billington (13)
Baverstock Specialist Sports College And Foundation School, Druids Heath

My Life

'Twas the winter of '91,
A cold and bitter day.
A woman was rushed to hospital,
A baby was on its way!

Ten painful hours later,
A baby girl was born.
Her parents were overjoyed,
As they watched a new life dawn.

I've lived in many places,
And now as time's gone on,
I look back on thirteen years,
And wonder where it's gone.

So my advice to you is,
To live life to the full,
To cherish every moment and,
To make life not so dull.

Bethany Prottey (13)
Baverstock Specialist Sports College And Foundation School, Druids Heath

A Usual Sunday Morning

It was an early Sunday morning
I did not know what I was doing.
But as soon as I got out of bed,
Football was in my head.
I got a ball and scored a goal,
And then I scored one more!

When my dad marched down the stairs
It was then he told me,
'You are in the England squad my son
For that I'll send you a pair.'

No way I cannot believe it,
But first back to my pit!
And tomorrow when I wake,
I'll turn up in my kit!

Finally the day has come,
But a red card in the third minute,
I walk off in shame.
The end of my career has come,
Right after the first game I played.

Spencer Walters (12)
Baverstock Specialist Sports College And Foundation School, Druids Heath

Hockey Ballad

Running down the hockey pitch,
Sticks hit with a clash,
Ball flies through the air,
Tooth shatters with a smash.

Blood dripped upon the sandy floor,
Drip, drip, drip,
Broken tooth fell to the ground,
Hands rushed to her lip.

Shaky legs as she collapsed,
Knees fell to the floor,
Sand exposed to the bruises,
Sores hurt even more.

Frantic nurse comes running up,
Bandages at the ready,
Helps the poor girl to her feet,
Now she's standing steady.

Lisa Coleman (13)
Baverstock Specialist Sports College And Foundation School, Druids Heath

My Inspiration

To me, she is the greatest woman on Earth.
Ever since the day she gave birth,
Not just to me, but my siblings as well.
On her agonising past, she did not dwell,
Even though she was put through hell,
She stayed strong,
Through all the hate
But to this pain, I can not relate.
Their retaliation,
Was her motivation,
To make it through and rise above.
Strength, is my mother,
For all of her love.

Zahra Serish (15)
Bordesley Green Girls' School, Birmingham

Wondering About Growing Up

As my eyes wander down the map,
I think of how I will grow up,
Suddenly, I hear my friends chattering away,
If growing up means leaving them,
I have forgotten all about the happiness of growing up,
You've probably realised I'm only 9 or 10,
Miss Willson comes by and says, 'Get on,'
I reach out for my pen, realising of all things,
Being in a classroom will never be the same,
As soon as I am up and out of a child's life,
Doing all sorts of grown-up things,
I open my eyes as much as I can,
Trying to memorise as much as I can,
I look around and see,
Memories which will always last with me,
I see tables, chairs, Miss Willson's face bobbing,
Up, down and all around.
I look around and see shelves of colourful boxes,
I glance over to the board, see the set work,
And try taking a picture of it in my mind.
I blink and then I'm suddenly looking outside the windows,
I hear the teachers shouting, telling everyone to pack away,
But I feel better when I stay in the class,
Admiring all of the displays, computer work,
And much more that I don't see at home.
If only this wish came true and I didn't have to grow up.

Saima Jabeen & Tabassum Hussain (12)
Bordesley Green Girls' School, Birmingham

What You Are To Me

I am a scarlet rose; you are my jagged thorns,
clutching to me, protecting me.
I am the fiery sun; you are my intense rays,
helping me to outshine and to be all that I can.
I am a lake; you are my water,
filling me with ideas, dreams and hopes for the future.
I am a tree, you are my olive leaves,
sharing who and what I am
and becoming an important part of my life.
I am a heart; you are my beat,
beating rhythmically to my happiness,
my fear, my sadness, my excitement.
I am me and you are with me,
to share all that I am,
to share love, life, and happiness.
'Love is happy, love is fun
Love is warm as summer's sun,
Love is a blessing sweet and rare
Love is the joy two lovers share'
From the word I have written, I hope you see,
You make up everything that's part of me.
I love you more than these words can say
I love you more with each forthcoming day
I love you whether far or near
I love you more with diminishing fear . . .

Always . . .

Shamala Tamasar (16)
Bordesley Green Girls' School, Birmingham

Blood Vs Bullet

(The Trenches)

Rainstorms blasted through,
Nothing to do, only me and you.
Not a minute of sleep,
Because you're thinking so deep.
One night in a muddy bed,
Next it's a bullet through your head.
You're surrounded with pitch-black coal;
Your bones settled down the defence hole.
You not breathing is their aim.
Dead cold blooded or in a fatal flame.
Drops of blood swim down your skin,
The pain of your head stabs like a pin.
Scars and cuts come instantly your way,
There's no stopping, they're here to stay.
Your own country, is where you show respect,
You succeeding has a great effect.

Shadna Hussain (15)
Bordesley Green Girls' School, Birmingham

Diana The Princess Of Wales

Diana the Princess of Wales
Was naive, young and beautiful
Who was married to the Prince of Wales

The Princess of Wales loved supporting every charity
She was keen and went to several countries to help
The homeless Aids sufferers
The only thing she wanted to see was happiness everywhere.

The day of her death was 31 August 1997,
Many people were in shock after hearing the news
For many people it was unbelievable to hear about her death,
Goodbye English rose.

Asma Khanam (15)
Bordesley Green Girls' School, Birmingham

Memories Of Primary School

Waking up in the morning to go to school
Hair tucked in, clothes ironed, I'm really cool
On my way I smell shaved grass
I hurry up before the bell rings to class

My teacher greets me with a great smile
Oh how I missed that for a while
Putting my school bag away
Getting my book out for the lesson today

The laughing bell rings
Chattering children hurry to the playground to get to the swings
On my way to the library
I pass the colourful corridors and there's a photo of me

We line up, it's time for dinner
We smell the chips and burgers simmer
We eat the food, gobble it up
We wash it down with orange or pop

Next we do art all afternoon
I draw a town, it's night with a shining moon.
Oh no it suddenly strikes me
The thing I've been dreading has come so quickly, how can it be?

I'm moving on to a new place
It's the last day and what can I say
Primary school, I spent all my life here
Now I'm moving, couldn't I just stay for another year?

What a step to take
What a bound to break
Primary school you're in my heart with me
I'll never forget you for eternity

I'll be missing you
In my heart you'll always be true
Now as I think of primary school in my bed
Memories come buzzing in my head

I'll never forget you . . . will you forget me?

Reham Badawy (12)
Bordesley Green Girls' School, Birmingham

The Big Bang

It's a cool day,
Totally relaxed in the middle of May.
Sitting alone,
Just where I belong.
Thinking of a theory,
On how I can prove gravity.
Whoosh! Bang! Ouch my head!
An apple just fell in the rose-bed.
My answer, my solution, that's just great,
Could have been fate,
That I was sitting under that tree,
Or it could have been destiny,
When I discovered the answer to gravity.
Now I'll be famous,
Maybe even glamorous?
It just goes to show, I, Isaac Newton have a great mind . . .

Naemah Tariq (14)
Bordesley Green Girls' School, Birmingham

Mum

The three letter word,
How she went through pain and hell,
To bring me to this wondrous world.
She cares for me like no other,
I love her so dearly,
Thanks for believing in me.
To me love is a word
To her it's a feeling.
She was there for me every step of the way,
She clothed and fed me every day.
Thank you Mum for all you've done
For being the one person I can trust
Whenever, wherever Mum,
I'll love you forever.

Sonia Nawaz (14)
Bordesley Green Girls' School, Birmingham

My Mum

Once I was your little girl
and how you cared for me
you gave me love and tenderness
and you taught me who to be.
You watched me grow and learn
caught me when I fell
encouraged me to do my best
even though I didn't do that well.
Now I am a growing woman
you are still her for me
supporting me in all I do
and yet allowing me to be free.
The love I have for you
no word could ever say
you have made me everything
and I'm thankful every day.
You're not just my mum, you're my best friend
I'll love you always Mum.

Sofia Bano (14)
Bordesley Green Girls' School, Birmingham

My Mum

My mum is the best ever,
No one can beat her no, no, never!
She makes me delicious pancakes for tea,
She is always there for me.
When I am poorly she is there by me,
No matter how sick I am, she is there for me.
I love my mum, I hope she loves me,
We are the best of friends for eternity,
My loving, caring mother there for me,
Her name engraved in my heart deep down,
She has an exquisite personality,
My loving, caring mother is always there for me.

Taiba Rafiq (14)
Bordesley Green Girls' School, Birmingham

Sports!

Sport, sport we do it every day,
Sport, sport we love to play.

We play football all day and night,
So we don't get into a big massive fight.

I play hockey and win the game,
It's so exciting but never the same.

When we play netball we love to shoot in the hoops,
When we shoot it does a loop the loop.

We play sport indoors and out,
We run around and about.

We do PE whether it rains, snows or when it is hot,
We do PE and we love it a lot.

When we win the game,
Everybody goes insane!

Salmah Begum (12)
Bordesley Green Girls' School, Birmingham

Who Am I?

Plays and poems are what I used to write
My plays live on even though I have died
The plays that I've written are now loved by you
Writing plays is my talent, and poems too.
I'm remembered by you now that I'm dead,
Otherwise I could charm you by my looks
I'm history now, a theme that you're taught,
My poems are still here, living on.
The plays I've written are now acted out,
My poetry of Earth will never die
My poems are from experiences
I'm the one who wrote that play, Twelfth Night
Macbeth and Othello I wrote them too
You should know me by now, this is my last line.

Mevish Hanif (14)
Bordesley Green Girls' School, Birmingham

The Great Mind

I know of a mind
that thinks like no other
it learns from one
and teaches another

Loving and caring
Its intelligence is extreme
Thinking and knowing
Its knowledge is supreme

The mind has no empty spaces
It's full of inspiration
Its effort is at its highest
Showing this through dedication

It makes decisions very carefully
Like calculating a sum
But I surely know that
This great mind belongs to my mum.

Asha Khanum (13)
Bordesley Green Girls' School, Birmingham

George Cadbury

George Cadbury was a coffee dealer,
Then he soon became a confectioner,
He opened a chocolate factory
And this made him gain such a victory.

The famous factory was named Bourneville,
This took place according to his own will,
He, George, and his brother worked together,
And this made the success even greater.

Soon after, George Cadbury passed away,
But still chocolate increased every day,
Bourneville is now named as Cadbury World,
Because it is now spread around the world.

Zaynah Sayed Ackbar (13)
Bordesley Green Girls' School, Birmingham

Friends

A friend is a treasure
And is always there for you
When you feel low
A friend is someone you turn to

A friend is like the sunshine
That brightens up your day
They are honest with you
In each and every way

A friend is helpful and polite
Someone who is nice and caring
They are always there for you
And are faithful and sharing

A friend is someone who fills our lives
With beauty, joy and grace
And makes the world we live in
A better and happier place.

Samina Kauser (13)
Bordesley Green Girls' School, Birmingham

Wondering

He's gone for a long time but don't know where,
Don't know why he's left me to cry.

I wonder when will my eyes rest from tears
And when will my heart stop bleeding
And when will I seek peace?

I feel like a piteous bird in a cage
Oh how I want to spread my wings and fly.
As I gaze outside the window I see people
Walking happily, children laughing and playing.
Why are the problems thrown in my direction?

All I'm left to do now is sit, wait and wonder,
When will he return and when will I rest my weary
Head and my teary eyes?

Mahvesh Mahmood (13)
Bordesley Green Girls' School, Birmingham

Shattered Reflection

(Inspired by Marilyn Monroe)

Standing alone, yet surrounded by cameras,
Wallowing in treacherous misery,
Hidden behind red lips and blonde hair,
Waiting for a saviour to rescue me
From this sinking ship called fame.
This façade can no longer go on,
Smothered in pain and sorrow,
I will almost certainly suffocate
In shame and disappointment,
Hidden behind red lips and blonde hair,
Waiting for a saviour
To rescue me from this sinking ship called fame.
Glamour and riches are nothing
Compared with a broken heart,
Shattered and drowning in
A river of empty promises.
Gazing at the face of a stranger in the mirror,
Hidden behind red lips and blonde hair,
Waiting for a saviour to rescue me
From this sinking ship called fame.

Lailah Said (14)
Bordesley Green Girls' School, Birmingham

Friends Forever

Friends are there forever,
That's why us four friends,
Stick together in good or bad times,
Nothing or no one can tear us apart,
No silly arguments, frights or rumours will part us,
Because we are four pieces of the same jigsaw,
Stuck in each other's hearts,
Friends are there forever.

Faiza Iqbal (12)
Bordesley Green Girls' School, Birmingham

The Younger And Older Days

Remember the times we were younger than young,
The times when laughter would be heard,
The days when you would rush into class if you were late,
But there is no doubt, Miss would always shout
Or say any angry words.

See now that I'm a little bit older than younger,
There are no more bright displays gleaming with yellows or greens.
Instead I see dullness surrounding me,
With lifeless colours worse than are ever seen.

What happens in my life when I'm at my oldest point
Of being a teenager?
I'm positive there'll be no teacher at college
Greeting me with a welcoming smile,
I've got an idea, I think I'll write back when I'm older than old,
That should be a while!

Badam Neewa (12)
Bordesley Green Girls' School, Birmingham

Life Is Unfair!

These are the clothes that my big brother wore,
And his elder brother and his before,
These are the short pants which reach to the floor,
For I'm much shorter than the one before.

This is the hat that he no longer wears,
He has big brothers and now he wears theirs,
The socks I have are in non-matching pairs,
And the tops have sleeves full of holes and tears.

This is the sole of my big brother's shoe,
His brother wore it and his brother too,
These are the clothes that no rag-man would buy,
With holes through which any seagull could fly.

But I wear them and wish it was not me,
The youngest brother, who is known as Lee!

Yasmin Begum (14)
Bordesley Green Girls' School, Birmingham

The Greatest

He sang and rapped and all the rest
Just wanted to do the very best
I thought that maybe he was wrong
For some things said in his songs
But expressing feelings from inside
Was a way for him to confide
Voice out many answers and questions
And think up different suggestions
With artistic talent, and time
He produced great music and rhymes
Showing the world that people with different races
Culture, backgrounds and faces
Could also have the ability to dream
And do anything, even if possible it did not seem
All that is needed is determination and an open mind
To explore the world and maybe find
That special something that is needed
To have a great mind like Tupac, who succeeded
So thank you Tupac for showing us the way
To a better, brighter future someday.

Samina Shareen (14)
Bordesley Green Girls' School, Birmingham

Friendship

F orever friends
R emembering each other forever and ever,
I ntelligent as can be,
E yes are tired when we play (Do not blink or you will lose)
N ever ends our fun and delight,
D ancing and singing,
S pecial friends care for one another,
H aving fun all night through,
I n your mind your friends will stay,
P laying lots of different games.

Aksa Hussain (12)
Bordesley Green Girls' School, Birmingham

Mind Of War

And here, this frailty
Embeds glass salt in her wounds
To bring forth a change
Towards fear of men, in vain.

His anger intensifies, and . . .
Down goes another one; end
. . . an unfinished day . . .
And start, filthy beast-like play.

He falls, and rises . . .
On the cut of the jugular,
As a sacrifice?
For he, like sheep, ask but why?

And here ,this frailty
Black blood blemished her soil
She, nature, in grief
To watch at the edge of war.

Great minds, fail course of action
. . . An unfinished day, once more.

Sidrah Hussain (14)
Bordesley Green Girls' School, Birmingham

Best Friends

Best friends
Understanding
Caring, sharing, trusting
Giving and also receiving,
Friendship.

Umi Kulsoom (14)
Bordesley Green Girls' School, Birmingham

Reminiscence

To be loved, worshipped and adored, what a feeling
Shame it cannot be constant, I'm only a human being
Feelings inside of me are wasted
As other men and women are mated.

Why did it not last?
As I reminisce about the past
Trying to scrutinise and explain
As I speculate who is to blame.

Life carries on all the same.
With or without the flame
But to have such approbation
Must be fine in any situation.

I suppose . . . in my time,
I've had my share, of what was mine.

Humaira Begum (14)
Bordesley Green Girls' School, Birmingham

Missing You

As time goes on,
The emptiness grows,
I miss you more than anyone knows,
There's a place in my heart,
That is yours alone,
Which no one else can ever
Own
And if you keep me as a friend,
I'll keep you in my heart,
Lock it up and throw away the key,
So that no one else can ever take
You away from me!

Nafisa Iqbal (12)
Bordesley Green Girls' School, Birmingham

School, School

School is very cool,
So don't be a fool
Come to school
The dinners,
The games we play
In the playground.

So don't be a fool.
Do come to school.
Come to school.
Come to school.

School is cool.
School is cool.
At the school
There is a pool.

School is really cool
Don't be a fool,
Come to school.

Zainam Zaida (11)
Bordesley Green Girls' School, Birmingham

Friendship

F riends are very
R eliable,
I mportant,
E ncouraging,
N ever dishonest,
D elightful,
S weet,
H appy and never
I gnorant and sometimes a
P est,
S ometimes they can get a bit annoying too.

Savera Haroon (13)
Bordesley Green Girls' School, Birmingham

Primary School

Primary school is so cool
If you don't go there you're a fool
We used to have a swimming pool
We used to wear our kit
And jump in the pool to get nice and fit
Believe me, I used to go
Come and join in with the flow
You don't need any dough to say hello
Break was the best
Better than all the rest
You wouldn't get in trouble
But whatever you do
Don't burst the bubble
When the clock struck three
This was the time when you were free
So listen up
Now you know primary school
Is so cool
Don't be a fool
And miss primary school.

Nagina Akhtar (11)
Bordesley Green Girls' School, Birmingham

Light

Into the dim light, bare walls of my world,
You entered bringing light and life to me,
You are everything to me,
You are very kind and helpful too,
So make new friends and keep the old,
One silver, other is gold,
That's the wisest thing I've been told,
Our friendship has become a part of my life now,
It has its own special place in my life, heart and being,
So I thank you for the light, my friend!

Asima Ali (13)
Bordesley Green Girls' School, Birmingham

Primary School

The morning starts
The rain, the dark
The sun goes up
The moon goes down
Breakfast time
Next is school
It smells so cool, lime and fruit
PE, drama and even horror
Time flies
Dinner time smells like fries
Friends play games
You and I join in too
Ten past three
Home time now
I think I will get a gold star
So don't be a fool
Learning is cool.

Yasrath Begum (11)
Bordesley Green Girls' School, Birmingham

Friends!

You are my friend,
My companion,
Through good times and bad.
My friend,
My buddy,
Through happy and sad,
Beside me you stand,
Beside me you walk,
You are there to listen,
You are there to talk,
With happiness we stay.

Rahhe Ahmed (13)
Bordesley Green Girls' School, Birmingham

Little Miss Lonely

I'm Little Miss Lonely,
I have nobody.
I'm Little Miss Lonely,
I am the only.
I'm Little Miss Lonely,
I have no security.
I'm Little Miss Lonely,
I have no one to talk to.
I'm Little Miss Lonely,
I have no one to love.
I'm Little Miss Lonely,
I plea for your love and your security.
So help me I'm fearful of all the
People around me and the
Only person that can help is
You!

Ruksar Hussain (12)
Bordesley Green Girls' School, Birmingham

How Do You Think I Look?

Do you think I look stupid?
Do you think I look crazy?
Do you think I look pretty?
Do you think I'm lazy?
Do you think I'm funny?
Do you think I look sexy?
Do you think I'm posh?
Do you think I attract you?
Do you think I'm in love?
Do you think I don't care about people?
Do you think I'm overweight?
Do you think I'm modern?
Just tell me how I look, oh great mind.

Halima Begum (13)
Bordesley Green Girls' School, Birmingham

My Role Model

She was there for me from when life started
And was there with me when life felt heavy hearted,
She made me smile every time I frowned,
With her words of wisdom and harmonious sound,
She is unquestionably my role model
And is loving, caring and extremely humble.

She watches me fail and pass
And sincerely hopes my smile lasts,
She leaves all my tears in the past
And brings a charm that's quick and fast.
All she wants is to see me succeed
And knows undoubtedly when I'm deeply in need.

And she will indisputably be here for the time to come,
I don't know where I'd be without her today,
She is surely, indeed, my dearest mum.

Sofina Khatun (15)
Bordesley Green Girls' School, Birmingham

Friendship

A friend is a *treasure,*
A friend is someone we turn to,
When our spirits need a lift,
A friend is someone we treasure,
For our friendship is a gift,
A friend is someone who fills our lives,
With beauty, joy and grace,
And makes the world we live in,
A better and happier place.
Friendship.

Nabeela Khalid (12)
Bordesley Green Girls' School, Birmingham

What Am I?

What am I?
Shakespeare is always writing on me,
I know he has a great mind,
However, sometimes I can't tolerate it,
He is constantly writing on me, page after page,
Never-ending, his writing is so creditworthy.
He has a great mind; he can write sonnets, poems, plays,
Shakespeare has written so much,
Twelfth Night, Romeo and Juliet, Macbeth,
These are all his famous plays.
He has done so well,
People look up to him but he looks down at me.
Shakespeare is a name everyone recognises,
People adore him because of his talent,
I adore him too, if only he wrote on the carpets, walls
Or his head, anywhere except me.
But what am I?
I'm just a piece of paper, that Shakespeare is always writing on.

Sunum Begum (14)
Bordesley Green Girls' School, Birmingham

Friendship

Friendships you remember are placed in your heart,
Friends you remember are never apart,
They stick together just like paste,
But as long as we have friendship each day is never a waste,
New friends are new, old friends are old,
But new friends are silver and old friends are gold.
Friends! What are they?
It seems whatever a situation good or bad,
You can always rely on your friends
No matter how sad.

Kirren Arshad (12)
Bordesley Green Girls' School, Birmingham

Who Is He?

He has such a great mind,
Writing sonnets, ballads and plays.
He sometimes writes from experiences
Or totally from the top of his head.

People loved him, they still do.
He can irritate me sometimes with his rhyming couplets and
Iambic pentameter,
He is as clever as a cheetah,
I've never met him of course,
However, I've heard noble things about him.

He writes about love, hate, deceit,
Sometimes portrays women as the inferior sex.
He put me through anxiety during my SATs,
Now he's doing it again in my GCSEs.

He used irony and repetition to give us a clearer perspective,
Nevertheless we become flustered at different stages,
His dialogues have become platitudes,
His talent is sporadically everywhere,
He is an icon who people look up to.

I can guarantee he's stressed you out too, at least once,
Can you guess who he is?

Aneesa Begum (15)
Bordesley Green Girls' School, Birmingham

Happiness

I am happy when it is my birthday,
At home with my family,
Playing on the PC and in the garden very happily,
Pillow fights in the bedroom, splashing water in the bathroom,
Helping Mum and Dad at home,
Happiness is never to be alone.

Hannah Sultan (12)
Bordesley Green Girls' School, Birmingham

A Dozen Roses

The first rose holds the joy that's in my heart today,
The second is the feelings I feel in every way.

The third rose is the sunshine around me when you're near,
The fourth holds the shedding of every joyful tear.

The fifth rose is the patience in your heart for me at all times,
The sixth makes up for waiting for the words you love in rhymes.

The seventh rose holds the caring I give so full and free,
The eighth it holds the loving you give so much to me.

The ninth rose is to forgive me when I am harsh or wrong,
The tenth is to thank you for choosing me through your whole life long.

The eleventh rose is to say I love you each and every way,
The twelfth is to carry these feelings from day to day to day.

Another dozen roses, a dozen reasons shared,
Of love, life and friendship with my love who always cared.

I am asking you to be mine,
For this and every valentine.

Rahana Rafiq (12)
Bordesley Green Girls' School, Birmingham

Who Do You Think I Am?

I am a very important aspect of your lives,
Without me,
You would not survive,
I have a great mind,
Who I am, you probably shall not find,
I'm colourless, I'm odourless,
I'm highly reactive,
I am also quite happily active,
That's all I'm saying,
For the rest is for your mind's making!

Shabana Nazir (15)
Bordesley Green Girls' School, Birmingham

A Day In Year 6

First thing you smell when you walk through that door,
Is the lovely fragrance spreading around the room,
The sound of the teacher stamping her high heels on the floor,
Makes you wonder if you've got into some trouble.

You change your mind when she gives you her smile,
And when she sings along to the music playing,
You can't help looking around at all the colourful displays,
Or look out of the window at all the cars going by.

As the bell rings for break,
All the whispering starts among the class,
The teacher starts to raise her voice,
But then quietens and leads you out.

You come inside after the bell rings again,
For the end of break,
All the chocolates and crisps are put away,
A couple dropped on the floor.

You come back inside and the board's got some new writing,
You read it as you walk over to your seat,
You look around at some of your classmates,
To chat about what you're about to do.

The bell rings for home time,
Goodbye to your friends,
Tomorrow you will walk through that door,
To once again smell the fragrance.

Syeda Begum (12)
Bordesley Green Girls' School, Birmingham

The Happy Times

The happy times have gone forever,
The bright classroom will come back never,
The rustling of papers in the teacher's hands
And the 'sit down quietly' strict demands,
The screeching of the whiteboard pen,
Or if misbehaved, sent to the naughty den,
Then the loud bells would ring,
The sound of children packing away everything,
And that was just a part of the day.

Then the children would come running in,
Their faces bright with huge, wide grins,
At the sight of the milk tray, brought in for break,
Slurping sounds, as they drank, they would make,
The wooden chairs scraping the floor,
Of little boys asking for more,
The giggling of girls at rude remarks,
On the table left and the teacher's mad barks,
Those were the happy times,
Gone forever, gone.

Fouzia Rahman (12)
Bordesley Green Girls' School, Birmingham

Friendship

Some friends are separated by time,
Some by pride,
Some by differences and
Some by distances,
We may not see each other,
We may not be together,
We might not text or call each other.
But no matter how far or different we may be,
You'll always be a special friend to me!

Haneesa Khaliq (13)
Bordesley Green Girls' School, Birmingham

Love Is Something Not Nothing

Never whisper words of love,
If your feeling is not true,
Never look into one's eyes if,
You mean to break a heart,
Never say hello,
If you mean goodbye.

It has been scientifically proven
That sugar dissolves in water,
So please don't go out in the rain,
I can't afford to lose a sweet person,
Like you!

When your life is in darkness,
Pray to God and ask him to
Free you from darkness,
And if after you pray,
You're still in darkness,
Pay your electricity bill!

Suria Mahmood (13)
Bordesley Green Girls' School, Birmingham

Elizabeth

E lizabeth the Queen of England,
L and and power was her fame,
I independent queen she was,
Z ero tolerance against Catholicism,
A rtists painted portraits of her every day,
B ecause she was beautiful and strong,
E ducated and intelligent she was,
T hings she did, she did for England,
H er religion and faith were always for England.

Fatima Bibi (13)
Bordesley Green Girls' School, Birmingham

My Love For You!

Love is in the air,
You have to be fair,
You think your lover is cute,
But let's go and find a new dude.
You buy each other gifts,
Because you love them and think they're fit,
You want to get married,
But have second thoughts because you're worried.
Maybe you do have a reason for this, what you're doing,
But cannot understand the reason, your heart is breaking,
My love for you is the greatest treasure
Not just today but forever and ever,
My love for you will never go
For that even I did not know,
But I know you will always remain in my heart and mind,
Always so thoughtful and kind,
I will treasure the memories of our love,
Right until I am called to God above,
I love you more than words can say,
For in my heart you are always there,
Your smile, your laughs and your loving ways,
It will remain with me until my dying days,
Now it's time to say goodbye.

Rukhsahr Iqbal (12)
Bordesley Green Girls' School, Birmingham

Friends

F riends are forever,
R espect them for who they are,
I   ndeed they are intelligent,
E njoy the excitement,
D ream each night,
S how how much you care.
            For they are all you have!

Anisha Ali (13)
Bordesley Green Girls' School, Birmingham

Death

Before you die,
You might get to say goodbye,
To whom you love and care for,
Their hearts can be very sore,
Death is very hard to get through,
It is like a ship without a crew.

Halima Ali (13)
Bordesley Green Girls' School, Birmingham

I Am, I Am

I am rebellious,
I am independent,
I am superstitious,
I am a heroine,
I am ambitious,
But what do you think I am?

Rishma Khan (12)
Bordesley Green Girls' School, Birmingham

Sameena

S is for sensitivity,
A is for appearance,
M is for manners,
E is for energy,
E is for entertainment,
N is for naughty,
A is for angry.

Sameena Asghar (13)
Bordesley Green Girls' School, Birmingham

I Always Remember You

Whenever I switch on the television,
Whenever I go to bed,
Whenever I look in the mirror,
Or whenever I'm in the shed,
I always remember you.

Whenever I heat up a kettle,
Whenever I boil my tea,
Whenever I close the windows,
Or whenever I have a dream,
I always remember you.

Whenever I switch on the lamp,
Whenever I draw the curtains,
Whenever I wear my warm slippers,
Or whenever I put my shirt on,
I always remember you.

Whenever I do anything,
Whenever I see anything,
I always remember you,
Why?
Because I love you!

Aashiya Rahman (12)
Bordesley Green Girls' School, Birmingham

My Family

My mother thinks I'm rosy,
But my father thinks I'm nosy,
My elder brother thinks I'm mad,
My elder sister thinks I'm sad,
My little brother thinks I'm funny,
My little sister thinks I'm a bunny,
My baby brother thinks I'm a bear because I care.

Henna Parveen (13)
Bordesley Green Girls' School, Birmingham

Confucius

(Also known as Kongzi or Kung-Fu-Tzu) (551BC-479BC)

Life, gifted from God, precious and cherished.
Succeed to the best of your potential.
Illiteracy must all be perished.
Education can help make life simple.

Goals determine what you're going to be.
For talent is flame, genius a fire.
'Knowledge' is success' greatest key.
Art of learning you should all desire.

If you believe it, you can achieve it.
No one ever excused his way to success.
Study with pleasure but don't ever quit.
Do not get your life into a big mess.

Teach and learn for a good way of living.
Endeavour to lead a life for giving.

Muriam Butt (15)
Bordesley Green Girls' School, Birmingham

Skater Dude

He walked down the street
I'd seen him somewhere
His face stuck in my mind
And he made me stare.

He walked skateboard in hand
Hair flicking about
Then he stopped and still he did stand
Skateboard fell to the ground.

He flew down the street
Wind in his face
The dude was fast
Hair all over the place.

He went straight past me and through the door
I heard him ride away, I could see him no more.

Nicola Pedley (13)
Brownhills High School, Stoke-on-Trent

Stop The Extinction

Endangered animals are there to save,
Hunters, whalers and trappers aren't brave,
They kill for money and kill for fun,
The harpoon, net and deadly gun,
Trees get cut down, no home for birds,
The loss of their beauty can't be put into words,
Rhinos and tigers get shot for fun,
The number gets fewer after each day is done,
Sharks are deadly and kill to eat,
Men kill for fur as a luxury treat,
Animals are killed every day,
Varied from oryx to ocelot to okapi,
Extinction of animals in the world is real,
The problem won't go till we make it a big deal,
Elephants and zebras are also included,
For ivory and skin our ideals deluded.

Rachel Forrester (13)
Brownhills High School, Stoke-on-Trent

The Earth Sings

The waves shed tears as they flew swiftly through the air
like doves onto the sad beach,
as the smooth snow danced softly into the sea that weeps.
The earthquake's angry roar shook the ocean bed
with a vengeful scream,
as the fire of the jealous sun raced rapidly to the stream.
The sky blushed ruby-red as the wind sang
with an avalanche of fiery passion,
and the clouds glowed peachy pink with a heart
filled with love and depression.
The ozone tore itself apart in a storm of hurt that thunder felt,
as global warming burned the world
and made the crystal ice caps melt.

Natalie Leese (13)
Brownhills High School, Stoke-on-Trent

Minds

Everybody has brains,
They do not belong down drains,
People keep lots of intelligent thoughts,
That's the way they were taught.

Some people are very forgetful,
Although very intellectual,
Everybody is kind,
That's how you can tell they've got a good mind.

Rest your mind, go to bed,
When you wake up glowing ideas will pop from your head,
Lots of people do lots of thinking,
Use thinking to remember words for singing.

Concentration for best grades,
If your mind is weak you will fade,
Having a happy feeling inside your mind,
Is when you have an intention to do something.

Laura Pointon (13)
Brownhills High School, Stoke-on-Trent

Possession

You taunt me,
Leave me be,
Why can't you see
You're hurting me?

You have me in your possession,
You cause discretion,
You have an obsession,
You hate me you always mention.

I cry, I cry all through the night,
I'll probably even cry tonight,
I can't fight, I can't fight,
I want to see a bright light.

Jade Whitehouse (14)
Cradley High School, Halesowen

An Angel's Face!

What is that noise I can hear Mother
Up above in the attic so high?
Don't worry it's only your brother,
Don't be scared or afraid, don't cry.

What do you mean Mother?
Who is it that I've seen?
What are the shadows at night
That visit me in my dreams?

When you see the shadows
Don't be afraid, they will do you no harm.
It is only your brother watching over you
To keep you safe and warm.

I see the shadows catch my eye
But when I look they've gone.
A cold chill lingers in the air,
I know my time has come.

I close my eyes to fall asleep
And picture an angel's face.
Finally I can meet my brother
Up in Heaven the perfect place.

Hollie Foster (14)
Cradley High School, Halesowen

Amelia

When a newborn comes down to Earth,
How do you feel about a newborn?
Is it a boy or a girl?
You will find out soon enough.

How much does it weigh? Only the family knows.
The first time you hold him or her, isn't she beautiful?
You wonder if they will be OK.
The answer is yes.

Ashley Edwards (12)
Cradley High School, Halesowen

Scary

A creaky floorboard,
A frosty breeze,
A creepy noise,
Weak at the knees.

A mangled hand,
An echoing voice,
A skeleton staring,
Run! It's your choice.

Leave this house
And never come back,
Or I'll wake the dead
And they'll attack.

Run for your life,
Stabbing pains,
Sinking teeth,
Empty veins.

Now she's one of us,
You'll be next so rush, rush, *rush!*

Emma Wilkinson (13)
Cradley High School, Halesowen

Peace

I sit and watch,
Watch and sit,
Learning from the TV.

I can't believe how the day goes by,
Not a dream not a sigh.

If only no one bothered each other,
If only everyone had a mother,
If only everything we did was with ease,
In this world there would be peace.

Sohaib Qamar (12)
Cradley High School, Halesowen

Late Summer

The silence that falls across the hills
Is golden in colour, with pink and red
That flows forth from a dark horizon
To brightly marble the glowing skies.
Bonfire smoke from a distant home
Drifts above a viridian forest
That turns to scarlet with autumn's approach
And slowly fades as summer dies.
The scent of flowers on the breeze
Mingles with the leaves that float
Downwards to mix with loose dark earth
And lie at the mercy of the weather.
People and seasons always change
Friend to foe, and summer to autumn
Yet despite enemies and odd heavy rains
Memories of late summer stay forever.

Christine Stafford (14)
Cradley High School, Halesowen

I Wonder

I sit here and wonder,
Could things have been different,
We used to be friends,
Who knew it would all fall apart.

I sit here and wonder,
Why do you hate me now,
I didn't notice as things changed,
Then you just stopped talking to me.

I sit here and wonder,
If I will ever forgive you,
You made me feel so alone,
But now I'm happy and you're on your own.

Stefanie Davies (13)
Cradley High School, Halesowen

Something Is Happening To Me
Because Of Love

Something is happening,
Something is happening
Because of love.
Where I put the things I forget,
I alone am smiling
Because of love.
I like red roses very much.
I am very changed
Because of love.
I am thinking that I look nice.
I always look at the mirror
Because of love,
Because of love.

Huma Javed (13)
Cradley High School, Halesowen

Being You!

Don't change yourself for anyone,
Whoever they may be,
You only believe in who you are,
So please don't try and be me.

You are who you are,
There's no change in that,
So don't change yourself for anyone,
Even if you're thin or fat.

So be yourself,
Don't hide away,
Don't change yourself for anyone,
Whoever they are or whatever they say!

Aron Jones (13)
Cradley High School, Halesowen

Stone Cold

The dark grey walls,
The dying rose,
You forget his calls,
For flower buds close.

I thought you'd leave me be,
Your grief could never end,
You thought I'd never see
Your evil in the end.

I hope you had loved,
The same as I had,
My last words you shoved,
I'm sorry it made you sad.

This can never be,
I can't keep a hold,
I wish you would see
You make me stone cold.

Hayley Nock-Radford (12)
Cradley High School, Halesowen

Love

I love you,
The sun of my love.
We will never let go,
I will hold on tight.

I will be here for you,
Never forget you,
Then I said that you are a lovely person.

Katrina Haycock (13)
Cradley High School, Halesowen

How Can I Forget You?

How can I forget you?
You are my life,
The sun of my heart.

How can I forget you?
If you are the flower in the garden,
I wish I was a gardener,
To help you grow up.
If you are a magpie in the sky,
I wish I am your roost,
To give you warmth.
How can I forget you?
I wish I will accompany you forever,
No one can take the place of you.

How can I forget you?
Because the love is coming.

Carmen Phuah (13)
Cradley High School, Halesowen

The Snow

Snow, snow, wonderful snow,
When I wake up and look out of the window to see . . .
Thick snow and ice everywhere.
Freezing outside all day long.
The sleet! Loads of sleet coming down.
I put my clothes on and go outside,
I play with the snow all day.
I call for my friends to play
Snowball fights all day long.
When you feel your hands and feet freeze
Run a bath and dive in it.
Keep me warm under the water,
To feel your hands and feet come to life again.

Matthew Heathcock (12)
Cradley High School, Halesowen

A Letter To You!

Last week you broke my heart,
It made me very sad.
It's such a shame we had to part
And at the time you were mad.

I feel like I've lost everything,
I thought we were meant to be.
All I have left is my diamond ring,
You don't realise the hurt you brought to me.

I'm quite relieved the fight is over now,
They say that time will always heal,
Maybe in the future we can talk somehow,
The hurt and sadness that we feel.

I have so many things I need to say,
Maybe I'll send this to you
And you will read it some day.

Amy Cooper (12)
Cradley High School, Halesowen

Amy

She is my best friend,
She is always by my side.
She comes to my house,
She plays with me
But she always argues with me.
She is nice to me,
She sleeps over at mine.
I go shopping with her,
She calls for me.
She always trusts me,
She shares her secrets,
She has known me for a long time.
She gives me gifts,
She is my best friend for life.

Kirsty Bunn (12)
Cradley High School, Halesowen

Love

I love you with all my heart,
I am so glad we met,
I loved you from the very start,
Our love I'll never forget.

From the first day,
Till the very end
You stood by me through my debt
And gave me money I could lend.

I love it when I'm with you,
I don't like it when we're apart.
I don't know what I'd do
If you ever broke my heart.

Me and you together,
Hopefully we'll last forever.

Kelly Billingham (13)
Cradley High School, Halesowen

Love Is . . .

Love is great,
Love is a warm kiss,
Love is your soulmate,
Love is someone you always miss.

Love is on Valentine's Day,
Love is your best mate,
Love is not spending a day away,
Love is your greatest fate.

Love is waking to your lover's face,
Love is the one you want to kiss,
Love is never needing some space,
Love is a lover's bliss.

Love is what is meant to be,
Love is always you and me!

Laura Cadman (13)
Cradley High School, Halesowen

Anti Love

I didn't like it when I was with you,
That's why I had to let you go.
It wasn't working us two
So I had to let you know.

I know it hurt you so bad,
I didn't know what to say,
But now I'm so glad
Things went the other way.

Being friends means so much more,
It might not seem like it to you,
It might seem worse than it was before
But what was I meant to do?

Me and you together,
Staying friends forever.

Jade Fowkes (13)
Cradley High School, Halesowen

Shooting Stars

The countdown begins for a shooting star,
A comet speeds for shooting metal,
Out of sight within a few seconds,
Passing stars by the millions,
I'm looking for planets
When I'm racing with stars.

One and two I pass by planets,
I finish with Pluto,
I fly with comets,
Shoot with stars,
I'll land soon enough,
So jump with me,
Then sing with glee.

Matthew Plant (12)
Cradley High School, Halesowen

Love Is . . .

Love is . . .
Love is a warm feeling,
Love is patient,
Love is sticking together.
Love is . . .
Love is a Saturday night together,
Love is a morning full of kisses,
Love is when you sit together in the dark.
Love is . . .
Love is presents from each other at Christmas,
Love is when you feel like a saint,
Love is sitting on a bank at sunset.
Love is . . .
Love is a gift on your birthday,
Love is a night-time drink,
Love is silky blankets at dawn.
Love is . . .
Love is when your heart is on one person,
Love is sitting close watching a romantic film,
Love is giving a warm kiss before going away.
Love is . . .
Love is holding hands,
Love is best friends,
Love is really rare,
Love is . . .

Leanne Morgan (13)
Cradley High School, Halesowen

Cinderella

Cinderella lived with her ugly sisters,
She cleaned up after them,
Which gave her blisters,
She'd count them nine or ten.

Her stepmother received a letter
And so Cinderella heard,
That they were going to a ball, a get together,
The prince was looking for a girl.

They all went except Cinderella,
Looking all fancy and posh,
Trying to impress the fella,
'Cause they were all after his dosh.

Then Cinderella's godmother came
And thought her not going was a shame.
So she zapped her into a lovely dress,
As if she was ready for marriage,
She was looking her absolute best
As she stepped into her carriage.

Cinderella at last saw the prince,
She stepped down the stairs
And with him started to dance,
They were the perfect pair.

The music was floating,
The pair were dancing,
The ugly sisters were gloating,
The stepmother was prancing.
Cinderella and the prince got married with joy and laughter,
As they all lived happily ever after!

Faiza Salim (13)
Cradley High School, Halesowen

Motorcross

One day I woke up and stacked my trailer,
But then it was a failure.
When I got to the track I rode my bike
And then I took it on a long, long hike.

On the hike I fell in the mud,
Then it got all in my hood.
So I was wet and cold
And my bike looked really old.

I rode my dirty bike back
With some boys to the track.
Then we had some food,
But my bike was in a mood.

My bike wouldn't start,
So then I drove my cart.
When I got home I washed my bike
And the mud got all over my grandad, Mike.

Zak Horan (12)
Cradley High School, Halesowen

Dad

My dad is the best,
Better than all the rest.
When I'm on my dad's bike
He always gives me a fright.
When I'm with him I feel like I'm special,
When we play football I feel excellent.
He makes great Sunday dinners.
When I go on holiday I love it,
When I go I always miss him,
I feel part of me stays with him,
When we're together I feel whole.

Phillip Cook (12)
Cradley High School, Halesowen

The Stone Chamber

You curl up in the corner,
You don't know what to say,
Others know what to do,
But they hide it every day.

The tongue spoke the slanderous words
That got you in this mess,
That is your horrible life today
And made pain your house address.

Just as the butcher's carving knife,
That cut the dripping meat,
Are the murder, the murderous attitudes
Of vipers at your feet.

And on the messed up, cobbled wall
There is a written word,
'No freedom for those people lost
In this confusing world'.

Leah Jones (13)
Cradley High School, Halesowen

Bullying

They start in the day and stop in the night,
They catch you up and give you a fright.

They catch you up at the end of school,
Whatever they do they break a rule.

They punch you up and kick you down,
They turn your smile into a frown.

I'm writing this poem for the victims out there,
So ignore the bullies and please take care.

Michael Hickman (12)
Cradley High School, Halesowen

The Love Poem!

We met by chance,
Sexy looks and smiles
On a boat to France
With blue sea for miles.

Candlelit dinners
Set out for two,
This had to be a winner,
The sparks flew high, we both knew.

Chocolates, gifts and roses,
The weather's so cold,
Down on one knee he proposes,
So thin, so pale yet so gold.

It's now time for wine,
Wedding bells chime.

Rebecca James (13)
Cradley High School, Halesowen

Football

Football, football is the best,
I like it better than the rest.
When I play I'm just the best,
I kick the ball it lands in the goalie's chest.
The ball bounces here, there and everywhere across the pitch,
Up and down, it hits the net and makes me feel proud.

The crowd cry in enjoyment.
The score was 1-0 so Aston Villa in the lead with one goal.
Arsenal's players felt so miserable.
We shout and sway, jump and run in enjoyment.

I dribble the ball and tackled the players,
I was about to shoot, the goalie did a slide tackle and he fouled me.
Aston Villa had a penalty.
The crowd held their breath, I kicked it in the left-hand corner,
The crowds are shouting, Arsenal's players are fighting.

Abdulla Salam (12)
Cradley High School, Halesowen

Seaside

Whooshing waves
Speeding up the shore,
Give me pretty shells more, more and more.

Sandcastles, towers standing tall,
Waiting for the tide to make them fall
With its surf more, more, and more.

Ice creams cool and white,
If one gets spilt your mum'll have a fright,
Yum, yum, tasty more, more and more.

Cool surfers speeding around,
Not very happy when their boards hit the ground,
Big, big waves more, more and more.

Last of all come the big tall rocks,
Giving you bruises and nasty knocks,
Needing plasters more, more and more.

Matthew Jones (11)
Dayncourt School Specialist Sports College, Radcliffe-on-Trent

Leg Of Lamb!
(Inspired by 'Fishbones Dreaming' by Matthew Sweeney)

A leg of lamb
Eaten by a man,
Still burning hot, half-eaten,
He didn't want to be that way,
He shut his eyes and dreamt back.

Back to when he was
In the fields with his family,
Jumping around in the green fields,
Munching on green grass.

He liked it that way,
So he didn't close his eyes
Or dream back.

Katie Fletcher (11)
Dayncourt School Specialist Sports College, Radcliffe-on-Trent

Little Red Riding Good!

As Little Red Riding Good was cleaning the floor,
Grandma walked through the door,
She jumped on her feet and asked Grandma to have a seat.
Little Red Riding Good asked Grandma to go to town,
As she was going to a ball and needed a crown.
She looked in the most expensive shops,
But for some reason Grandma was hiding from all the cops.
Little Red Riding Good found a dress,
As she finished paying it all became a mess.
Grandma started to get chased down the street,
Not knowing she was showing her hairy feet.
Suddenly Grandma's clothes started to tear,
Only to reveal she was actually a bear.
She was going to ring her mum to see if she could take her home,
But then she found out the bear had nicked her phone.
So she had to catch the bus,
Making such a fuss.
When she got home she got in her new dress,
Looked in the mirror and said, 'What a success.'
She got picked up by a horse and carriage
And on the way home she was arranging a marriage.

Ria Mills (11)
Dayncourt School Specialist Sports College, Radcliffe-on-Trent

Trees!

Branches bang like they're knocking on the door,
All the leaves flutter to the floor,
Trees stand bare
Like they just don't care.

They wave all around
And they listen to the sound
Of all the birds flying
And all the people sighing.

Wonder what it's like to be a tree,
Not being able to break free.

Victoria Coates (12)
Dayncourt School Specialist Sports College, Radcliffe-on-Trent

Football

I love you, you're the best,
When I score I give you a rest.
I kick you with so much curl
Because you are my diamond pearl.
You've got white and black patches
And you win me the matches.
I love you so much, football
That's why I kick you against the wall.
I always take part
Because I love you with all my heart.
Now please win me the games
Because my name's not James.
I put you on the spot
And I never lose the plot.
I place you in the bottom right
And celebrate with all my might,
I love you football.

Chris Marshall (12)
Dayncourt School Specialist Sports College, Radcliffe-on-Trent

Chicken Tonight
(Inspired by 'Fishbones Dreaming' by Matthew Sweeney)

On the farm with his friends,
People looking at him and feeding him,
Eating a pile of corn.

He liked to be this way,
Eating corn until dawn.

Mum is making dinner,
The smell of chicken on the stove.

He didn't like to be this way,
He shut his eyes and looked away.

Lovely dinners for me and you,
Eating every bit of food,
But he didn't eat his corn.

Natalie White (12)
Dayncourt School Specialist Sports College, Radcliffe-on-Trent

Little Miss Prim

Little Miss Prim went walking one day
And there in the wood a wolf did stray.

She knocked on the door with a rat-a-tat-tat,
The wolf jumped out of bed and said, 'Who is that?'

'It's me,' cried Miss Prim, 'I'm going to the fair.'
'Oh are you,' said the wolf, 'then I'll follow you there.'

When she got to the fair, on the coconut shy
She threw a coconut and hit the wolf's eye.

Steam came out of the wolf's ears,
As Miss Prim was sadly in tears.

Little Miss Prim ran back into the wood,
With the wolf following as fast as he could.

While Little Miss Prim was trying to hide,
Out of a bush came Miss Whiteside.

They came to a bridge in the next hour,
But they then spotted Rapunzel's tower.

The wolf still chasing faster and faster,
Miss Prim and Miss Whiteside were in a disaster.

They came to the tower and climbed the hair,
The wolf still behind, would the wolf dare?

The wolf did dare to climb the hair,
But in a tick he wasn't there.

'I've cut it,' Miss Whiteside said
And in the lake the wolf was dead!

Emily May Woodhouse (11)
Dayncourt School Specialist Sports College, Radcliffe-on-Trent

Little Red Riding Hood

Little Red Riding Hood loves to fly,
She flies so high but is so shy.
In her bright red dress
She looks the best.
But the only thing she doesn't know,
Wolfie's around shouting po.
Her grandma has sent her on a mission,
While she's busy cleaning her kitchen.
Mr Wolf has seen her flying so high
And he thinks it's such a sight.
He's following her now
And he's going to eat a cow.
Wolfie likes eating little girls,
That's why he's in such a whirl.
Little Red Riding Hood is looking for a wand
And at the moment she can hear a band.
She's got the wand,
Her mother's going to be so proud.
Wolfie's decided not to eat the girl,
So he's following her with a twirl.
He then sees the mama
And he needs some supper,
He knocks on the door
And the grandma looks so poor.
He then gobbles her up,
With such a cup.
Little Red Riding Hood had such a fright
And it was a horrible sight!

Leah Woodford (12)
Dayncourt School Specialist Sports College, Radcliffe-on-Trent

Chicken Drumstick!

(Inspired by 'Fishbones Dreaming' by Matthew Sweeney)

Chicken Drumstick in a grubby rubbish bin,
Waiting silently in despair for cats to finish him off.

He didn't like to be this way,
He closed his eyes and thought back,

Back to when he was in the oven,
Sweating buckets and smoking a golden brown.

He didn't like to be this way,
He closed his eyes and thought back,

Back to when he was sitting on the kitchen counter,
Being plucked of his feathers covered in goosebumps.

He didn't like to be this way,
He closed his eyes and thought back,

Back to when he was in the slaughterhouse,
On a block of wood with bloodstains on the wall,
With an axe being held above his neck.

He *really* didn't like to be this way,
He closed his eyes and thought back,

Back to when he was with his friends,
In the lush green fields eating grain,

He liked to be this way.

Claire Leivers (12)
Dayncourt School Specialist Sports College, Radcliffe-on-Trent

Red Riding Hood

There was once a little girl, Red Riding Hood,
Who always did as she should,
Until one day she thought she'd be,
Rather naughty as you shall see.

Her mother gave her a job to do,
Go to Grandma and be back by two.
The bag she did go get,
But she was still watching the TV set.

She went out the front door,
The bag dragging on the floor.
She went to the shops to get a sweet,
But all they had was boiled meat.

Humpty Dumpty sat on the wall,
Red Riding Hood came and made him fall.
She had fried egg
And a freshly boiled chicken leg.

She went to the wood,
Doing this bit, as she should.
She found Grandma,
Who had just been shopping at the Spar.

She gave Grandma the heavy parts,
Who put them in her shopping carts.
Grandma made a tank
And played a prank.

She blew Red Riding Hood up right there,
As Hoody sailed through the air
Grandma said,
'Serves her right.'

Jonathan Horn (11)
Dayncourt School Specialist Sports College, Radcliffe-on-Trent

I Met Love

I met love,
His name is Valentine,
He has a warm and gentle touch,
His handshake filled me with joy . . .
As he gave me a kiss I cried,
He gave me a box and roses fell at his feet.
He gave me a box of chocolates,
I popped one into my mouth, *mmm!*
Lovely treat ran down my throat - delicious.
We danced across the waterfront and at 6.30
He ran away saying, 'The box, the box.'
I replied, 'What box?'
No answer.
As I carried my bruised and broken heart back home
I glanced at the box he had given me,
As I opened the box I could feel him watching over me,
I lifted the lid,
I found a necklace numbered 14.

Hanna Hulme (13)
Dayncourt School Specialist Sports College, Radcliffe-on-Trent

Meeting Winter

Her hair was as white as snow,
Her lips as red as blood,
Her touch as cold as ice,
Her fingers as slim as twigs from a tree.

> Her eyes were as blue as the sky,
> She had a robin that sat on her shoulder.

She lived in a little log cabin
In the middle of a frosty forest.

Kara Forrest (13)
Dayncourt School Specialist Sports College, Radcliffe-on-Trent

My Teeth

I like to brush my clean white teeth,
I like to brush my teeth.
And every week I count my teeth
And see they're sterling white.

In a month I'll paint my teeth
To stop them going yellow.
Everyone will look at me and think
Hey! Who switched that light on?

Eventually I'll get on the news
For having such white teeth.
Across all front covers you'll see my teeth,
Even in movies they'll be the star.

When I'm old I'll get good dentures,
They'll be sterling white too.
Then in old people's mags you'll see
Me, starring my new teeth.

Jack Cox (12)
Dayncourt School Specialist Sports College, Radcliffe-on-Trent

Spring

I met Spring one weekend,
Her hair was long, wavy and blonde.
Deep blue eyes sparkled upon her face like sapphires,
Her short, flowery dress blew in the gentle breeze,
In her hand she held a bouquet of flowers.
I followed her until she came to a stream bubbling happily,
Another girl stood near by,
They both laughed sweetly and smiled at each other,
Spring stepped into the stream and vanished,
Summer was here.

Sarah Gell (13)
Dayncourt School Specialist Sports College, Radcliffe-on-Trent

Rainforest

I open my eyes and see
A great green wonderland
Full of amazing animals
Who need a helping hand.

If I blink and look again
I get a great big shock
Because that big green paradise
Is gone with one big chop.

I look around and all I see
Is tree stumps and dust,
No living creatures there at all,
It's all gone without a fuss.

I mainly pity the animals
Who now have no home,
Most have lost their family
And now they are alone.

But what you do not realise
Is it's affecting you,
The planet's slowly heating up
And we must stop it too.

It isn't just the rainforest
Being chopped down,
It's also the pollution
That's happening in the towns.

So we must try and stop
The pollution that's happening,
To do this we must do a lot,
We must do everything.

Elizabeth Winter (12)
Dayncourt School Specialist Sports College, Radcliffe-on-Trent

The Sun

He lights up the day,
The bright blond boy
Working without any pay.

1 million years old,
But as fit as a fiddle,
Stuck in the middle
Of the great blue sky.

Slowly moving across the sky,
As he comes down,
The purple, pink colours
Shine all around.

Beaming and bouncing
Across the land.
He goes to rest
In the black night's sky.

Rebecca Gill (13)
Dayncourt School Specialist Sports College, Radcliffe-on-Trent

Chocs

Into the half a pound box of Dark Light
My creepy hands crept,
There was a Caterpillar's Crunch,
There was a dark horrible scent.
Into my open gross mouth
The first Wormy Whirl went,
Down in the creaking second layer
Five fingers found Beetle Juice
And Bee Sting, the Finger Swirl,
The Black Eyeball and a Rotten Nail,
But the last in the box is Snail Crust.

Ryan Geere (12)
Dayncourt School Specialist Sports College, Radcliffe-on-Trent

Me

My name is Aaron Denham,
I am thirteen years of age,
I'm of small build
And very strong-willed
And I don't like anger or rage.

I have blue eyes
And brown fair hair
And I'm always very happy,
But according to my friends
I'm more renowned as being snappy.

I live in an ex-mining village,
Cotgrave is its name,
It is very small
With a village hall,
But to me villages are all the same.

There are many shops to
Choose from, pets to DIY,
A grocery store which is a must
As these you have to buy.

Aaron Denham (13)
Dayncourt School Specialist Sports College, Radcliffe-on-Trent

Star, Oh Star

Star, oh star, burning bright,
There you shoot through darkest night,
Up at the sun you openly gaze,
As planets and rocks are lost in a maze
Of meteors and junk floating by,
They watch you as you swiftly fly
Through the wide open plains, that are space,
Gliding past the moon's round face,
Star, oh star, I love you so,
All I wanted, was to let you know.

Abi Kennie (12)
Dayncourt School Specialist Sports College, Radcliffe-on-Trent

Spring

Spring comes skipping happily along the lane,
Her long blonde hair blows in the wind.
She carries a basket that has flowers in,
She puts the flowers in all the gardens.
She brings baby animals,
She wears a light blue dress and blue sandals.
She sits in a field stroking lambs.
Everyone loves her.

Adele Goodwin (12)
Dayncourt School Specialist Sports College, Radcliffe-on-Trent

Dogs

Dogs are cute, dogs are cool,
But I don't like those dogs that always drool.

Dogs do this, dogs do that,
Dogs go wild when you say the word 'cat'.

Dogs like walking, but love to run,
Greyhounds speed when they hear the sound of a gun.

Dogs are da best, dogs are back,
I especially love my own dog, he's called Mac!

Joe Perkins (12)
Dayncourt School Specialist Sports College, Radcliffe-on-Trent

Sunset

I met Sunset,
She was warm and beautiful,
Everyone would stop and stare,
She was full of passionate colours,
She changed in looks every time I saw her,
She is never around in daytime,
But that's fine, I'll see her tonight.

Lauren Stevenson (13)
Dayncourt School Specialist Sports College, Radcliffe-on-Trent

Dustbin Lids!

Could you ever care for a dustbin lid?
Sitting poor as a cover.
Could you ever care for a dustbin lid?
Not a friend or a sight of a lover.

So what if it's blown in a crashing storm?
So what if the lid was even born?
Could you ever care for a dustbin lid?
No way, no how, no never,
So what if it's not as rich as leather,
No way, no how, no never!

The bricks don't care,
The shed won't stare,
Why care for a lid so cold and bare?
Could you ever care for a dustbin lid?
No way, no how, no never.

Rachel McDermott (12)
Dayncourt School Specialist Sports College, Radcliffe-on-Trent

Bullies

They hurt you in so many ways
By shouting, hitting and calling you names.
They don't care about what they do,
They won't stop hurting you.

People take it emotionally
And some are even serious.
Some will cry, cry and cry
And some will want to die.

People say you're nothing,
Even though some may be bluffing.
Some say no one likes you
And then they say are you gonna cry well boo hoo!

I should know you see
Because it happened to me . . .

Joseph Mascia (11)
Dayncourt School Specialist Sports College, Radcliffe-on-Trent

Monday

I met Monday,
His eyes were dull,
His face was dull,
He was dull.

Disliked by everyone,
Only very few times he brought happiness,
Just the odd occasion,
The rest of the week hated him.

He was old, boring and ugly
As Friday had once said to me.
He ambled past me,
The wind blowing on his ear hair.
He nodded at Tuesday
Who ignored him and went on her way,
'Miserable sod,' he muttered.

Evie Stannard (13)
Dayncourt School Specialist Sports College, Radcliffe-on-Trent

Spring

Green and blue and yellow of spring
This is where life will begin.
Blue birds twitter, little lambs run
All of the children having fun,
Laughing and joking, singing too,
Spring is the time that life breaks through.
Skies of blue and fields of green
All of the happiness clearly seen.
Spring is the time to make amends,
Help fights and rivalries come to an end.
Let love and light lead you through,
Forgive and forget is what you must do.
Spring brings us light, shows us the way,
Helps us to find that happy day,
The day that we will finally see
Together we are meant to be.

Chelsea Launder (13)
Farnborough School Technology College, Nottingham

The Haunted House

When I'm in the haunted house
I hear the scuttle of a little mouse,
Drowned by the creaking stairs
And the clash of thunder in the night air.

I can hear the constant slamming of the broken attic door,
An eerie ghostly moaning coming from beyond the basement floor.
I can hear a distant church bell ringing
And the underwater church choir still singing.

I'm getting really, really scared,
I think I'm gonna burst out in tears.
I'm getting shivers up and down my spine,
An evil presence, now an evil sign.

Someone's writing on the wall,
Like a car my feet are stalled.
It's all in blood, I think it said,
Get out! Get out! Or to the Devil you will head.

Kayleigh Dickinson (12)
Farnborough School Technology College, Nottingham

Kayak Adventure

Kayaking down the River Trent,
An interesting journey unfolds,
You fall in,
A cry for help
And a mouth full of dirty water.

Capsize in a kayak,
A hand roll is handy
If your paddles are floating downstream,
And if they're not
Use them to get you back up and away.

Luke Needham (13)
Farnborough School Technology College, Nottingham

Friends Of Nature

Tall tree
Up in the sky,
Together we laugh
And we cry.
We live together
Through good and bad,
When you're here I'm happy,
When you're not I'm sad.

Bird in my tree
Building your home,
Together we live
And together we roam.
We all live together
And you can join our three,
Me and you
With the bird and the tree.

David Hopkin (12)
Farnborough School Technology College, Nottingham

The Forbidden Door

What lies behind the forbidden door?
Is there nothing or is there more?
Take a look and you will see
What its contents hold for you and me,
But I must warn you before you stare
What lies beyond is quite a scare.
Many unsuspecting victims have tried,
Yet many of those have died!
So go ahead and you will see
What its contents hold for you and me.

Tom Wells (12)
Farnborough School Technology College, Nottingham

The Snowball Fight

Snowballs flying in the air,
Kids getting wet but they just don't care.
Bang, my friend just took a hit,
Like a burning match just being lit.
Children around you dropping like flies,
A snowball funeral but no one dies.
They're surrounding me now, that's it, I'm done
Staring down the long end of a snowball gun.
They pull the trigger, it's speeding towards me,
Timber! I fall down like an old oak tree.
Oh well, down but no way near out,
This isn't the end of our snowball bout.

Snowballs were flying in the air,
Kids were getting wet but they just didn't care.
But spring came in, chucked poor winter out,
There was never an end to our snowball bout.

Ashley Richardson (13)
Farnborough School Technology College, Nottingham

Creatures

Johnny was a snail,
He wore a woolly hat,
A tartan vest,
button to his chest,
And was very, very fat.

His cousin Doug
Was a black and spotty slug
Who enjoyed the odd leaf or two.
He works on a farm,
Shovelling hay in the barn,
Mucking out the cows that go moo.

James Freeman (13)
Farnborough School Technology College, Nottingham

My Autumn Poem

Nights are growing longer,
The moon is watching over,
Days are growing shorter,
The wind howls even louder.

The leaves are getting older,
It's time to say goodbye,
The old lady watches sadly,
For her time is running out.

Memories come flooding back,
Of happy times gone by,
Kicking the crumpled leaves with joy,
Back in her childhood days.

Leaves fall bleakly to the ground,
Shrivelled crisp and dry,
Reminding the old lady,
Of her tired wrinkled self.

Autumn draws to a close,
Winter follows on,
The old lady's life fades away,
As the seasons carry on!

Laura Kirby (12)
Farnborough School Technology College, Nottingham

Every Weekend

Friday night, the terror begins.
The two of us trouble, thank God we're not twins.
All weekend we fight, like cat and dog,
The continuous shouting, his head's in a fog.
We cannot be quiet, we're on all the while,
No peace for the wicked, he's no time to smile.
At the end of the weekend, he's just about mad,
Thank God for Monday, all is quiet for Dad.

Kathryn Sargent (13)
Farnborough School Technology College, Nottingham

A Poem About Love!

One day at a time
Is one more day I shall wait,
For I hope you love me,
If *not,* my heart will break.

I love you so much,
Words cannot describe,
Luke, please love me,
Don't take away my pride.

I don't know who you love,
But I hope that one is me,
Because no one loves you
As much as me.

People think they love you,
But I know that isn't true,
But I agree that there will be no one
Loved as much as you.

Many people say
That there is only one love of your life,
And you are my only love,
My one and only white dove.

Karissa Brewster (13)
Farnborough School Technology College, Nottingham

Would You Bloblermand?

If I delete every last dob
And replace them with a few new klob
I wonder if you would bloblermand
But some I would make blime.
With the words they were blablacin,
I wonder if you would bloblermand
What on Earth I was kayin.

Megan Hobson (12)
Farnborough School Technology College, Nottingham

Winter Lives On

'It's over now,'
One's often said,
'Another season over,
Another season dead.'

But winter,
Oh! She's on the operating table,
They're trying to revive her,
This isn't a story or a fable.

It's the middle of February,
But it's still snowing,
Children throwing snowballs
Not knowing where they're going.

Oh dear,
Winter's coughing and spluttering,
Her once crisp ice
Thawed and down the guttering.

March now,
The spring's got the better of dear winter,
She was a good season,
Now until next year - she'll hit like a splinter.

'It's over now,'
One's often said,
'Another season over,
Another season dead.'

Alicia Leeanne Hoad (13)
Farnborough School Technology College, Nottingham

A Teenager's Life

Wake up, wake up! It's time for school.
A teenager's life can be so uncool.
Monday to Friday the same old thing,
Can't wait for the weekend, when freedom kicks in!

Books, papers, pens, uniform, are all part of school.
What us kids find hard is sticking to the rules.
We're at the age, not adult, not child,
A bit of a misfit that drives parents wild.

Our bodies are changing and so are our minds.
I've heard people say that we're not so kind.
We really don't mean some things that we do,
We're testing the world and testing you!

These changes are part of the big process,
We have to go through them before we progress
Into people that other people like.
We're trying to fit, to do things right.

Look on the bright side, there's a light at the end.
One day we'll grow up, and go round the bend,
For the troubles, the traumas, the dramas that you went through,
Cos one day we'll have teenagers and experience it too!

Kirstin Rowan (13)
Farnborough School Technology College, Nottingham

Tall Tree

Tall tree
Up in the sky
You stand so tall, though you started from a seed
We grow together
Side by side
I admire you
Your colourful green leaves
Your complicated twists and turns
Your withered skin looks just like mine
I admire you
I am growing old
Though you are not
And you still stand ever so bold
I will die long before you
And you will see my children grow
But when you die, come find me
And tell me dear, what you did see.

Ellie Sewell (12)
Farnborough School Technology College, Nottingham

Footballer's Jokes

Wayne Rooney is fast like a hare,
He kicks a football like a train in fast gear,
He uses tricky skills like a magic show.
When he passes the ball to his goalie,
He whacks the ball as if the goalie
Doesn't have enough strength to save the ball.

Reece Hutchinson (11)
Henry Mellish Comprehensive School, Nottingham

Jo-Jo

Jo-Jo's eyes are as blue as the sky,
Her nose is as big as the world,
Her hair is as stringy as a piece of string,
Her lips are as small as an unhappy ant,
She walks like a skittle that has just been knocked down,
Her voice is as low as the ground,
Her legs are as big as big, fat, wooden sticks,
Her toes are as big as an elephant's nose.

Jo-Jo's feet are windows,
Her lips are a big baboon.

Shelley Smith (11)
Henry Mellish Comprehensive School, Nottingham

My Role Model Is My Mum

My mum's eyes are as brown as can be,
Her nose is as pink as the Pink Panther,
Her hair is as soft as babies' skin,
Her lips are as red as a rose,
Her voice is as hard as rocks,
Her voice is as rough as sandpaper,
Her voice is as sweet as sugar,
She walks like a proud person.

Chantelle Watson (11)
Henry Mellish Comprehensive School, Nottingham

Snow - Haiku

Pure white and fluffy
Roll it up into a ball
Snowball fights begin.

Nyala Skerritt (13)
Henry Mellish Comprehensive School, Nottingham

Andrew M

Andrew M's eyes are as big as clocks,
His nose is as flat as a table,
His hair is as gay as a gay man,
He walks like a short man,
His lips are like bubbles,
His voice is as shallow as a baby pool,
His skin is like a rough floor,
His house is like a bin,
His head is as small as an ant,
He runs as slowly as a turtle,
He is as big as an A4 piece of paper,
His fingers are like a packet of sausages,
His feet are as long as a metre ruler.

Andrew M is a big white whale,
He is a mardy baby,
He is a cheeky monkey.

Levi Pollard (12)
Henry Mellish Comprehensive School, Nottingham

About Chantelle

Chantelle's eyes are as hazel as my cats,
Her nose is as pink as a dark pink car,
Her hair is like a brown cookie,
Her lips are like baby lips,
She walks like a vampire,
Her voice is as squeaky as a baby crying.
She likes sweets as much as her mum,
Her hands are as soft as a fur blanket,
She likes English as much as swimming.

Chantelle is a bad girl at school,
She is a bunch of mangoes in a tree.

Priscilla Chakana (11)
Henry Mellish Comprehensive School, Nottingham

Fern

Fern's eyes are as brown as curtains,
Her nose is as red as blood,
Her hair is like the bark on a tree,
Her lips are like a fish,
She walks like a stiff robot,
Her voice is as deep as a dog,
Her legs are as short as an ant's leg,
Her feet are as big as a giant,
Her nose is as pointy as Pinocchio's.

She is a small ant,
She is an invisible zombie that comes out at night.

Amie Godber (11)
Henry Mellish Comprehensive School, Nottingham

Scamp

Scamp's eyes twinkle like stars,
His coat is like fine silk,
His nose is as black as the night sky,
He's as much fun as a bat and ball,
He's as trustworthy as your best friend,
He is as soft as a teddy,
He is as brave as a lion.

Luke Ashcroft (11)
Henry Mellish Comprehensive School, Nottingham

Dark - Haiku

Darkness falls like doom
Enveloping misty dark
You can't see shadows.

Luke Brown (13)
Henry Mellish Comprehensive School, Nottingham

My Role Model Is Amie

Amie's eyes are as big as balloons,
Her hair is as long as hay sticks,
Her nose is as long as Pinocchio's,
She's like a little mouse.

Her hair is as shiny as the sun,
Her ears are like Dumbo's ears,
Her head is as big as an elephant,
Her teeth are as yellow as the sun so bright.

Amie is a tiny mouse with a squeaky, tiny, cute voice.

Danielle Bowler (12)
Henry Mellish Comprehensive School, Nottingham

50 Cent

His house is as small as a tin,
His hair is like a very big bush,
His bodyguard's as small as an ant,
50 Cent is like a big-headed monster,
50 Cent's nose is like Reece in my class,

He's a monkey,
He is a small ant.

Sam Butler (11)
Henry Mellish Comprehensive School, Nottingham

Limerick

A puddle plops in the rain
like someone is in a lot of pain
it is very cold
like your house is sold
like the barking of a Great Dane.

Chris McGuire (13)
Henry Mellish Comprehensive School, Nottingham

Limericks

There was a man called Ned
Who knew a man called Fred
They lived in a flat
They both wore top hats
And were poor so shared a bed.

There was a woman called Val
Who was lonely and had no pal
She was small and thin
Who committed no sin
Till she met a man called Sal.

There is a cat called Pat
Who is stripy, long and fat
She lives on the street,
Has spotted feet
And wears a bobbly hat.

There is a dog called Mark
Who lives in Noah's Ark
He is small and thin
With chocolate skin
And has a friend who is a shark.

Jordan Brandom (13)
Henry Mellish Comprehensive School, Nottingham

Shadow

As I look at the shadow,
All I see is black,
Black in its eyes as you see the shape,
Of what this shadow has become,
As the light comes, a black flicker hits the wall,
And at night the shadow's gone.
Then in the morning it seems to have come back.

Katie Bignall (11)
Henry Mellish Comprehensive School, Nottingham

Limerick

There was a man from Japan
who got hit by a transit van,
he went to Spain
to do it again
but got hit by a frying pan.

Kane McLean (12)
Henry Mellish Comprehensive School, Nottingham

Limerick

There was a young man from Spain
Who was a bit of a pain,
He used to smack girls' bums
'Cause he thought they were chums,
So they took him to court for a claim.

Sophie Sanderson (12)
Henry Mellish Comprehensive School, Nottingham

Water - Haiku

Dripping in the sink
Water dripping on the floor
Overflowing now.

Kim Gough (13)
Henry Mellish Comprehensive School, Nottingham

The Rain - Haiku

A wet winter day,
The drops bounce off the wet floor,
Then puddles appear.

Hayleigh Walker-Randle (12)
Henry Mellish Comprehensive School, Nottingham

A Perfect Summer Day

The roses,
as red as they can be,
children
playing happily.

The sun
beaming down in clear view.
The sky
beautifully blue.

The sea
coming in and out calmly.

A perfect summer day.

Marie Pearce (12)
Henry Mellish Comprehensive School, Nottingham

Limerick

There was a young girl from Spain
who fell out of a plane,
she ate all the food
so then she couldn't move
and went home on a train.

Victoria Fowler (13)
Henry Mellish Comprehensive School, Nottingham

Limerick

There was a man from school
who sat there and started to drool
so he ran out of class
forgot his hall pass
and never returned to his school.

Michael Tyers (13)
Henry Mellish Comprehensive School, Nottingham

The Basic Instructions

The basic instructions:
You must eat to live.
Food is for nutrition.
You are what you eat.

But what about birthdays and parties and treats?
Then gluttonous food is what you should eat,
Chocolate cake, jelly and ice cream in a dish,
Roast beef, roast chicken and battered fish.

A little for breakfast,
Lunch and tea.
These are the basics.
Abide and survive.

French, Italian and Spanish cuisine,
The gourmet diners prefer to eat lean.
Indian, Chinese, Mexican and Thai,
There's lot of food for you to try.

Want to keep fit?
Keep off the sweets.
Bad for your teeth.
Your dentist's not wrong.

Sizzling, bubbling and roasting hot.
Flame-grilled, southern-fried and in a pot.
Food that you love and food that you hate,
Food in a bowl and food on your plate.

Not too much salt.
Not too much sugar.
Eat more vegetables,
Five a day.

Afternoon tea and after-dinner coffee,
Sherbet, Mars bars, traditional sticky toffee,
Some people like seafood and some prefer steak,
It is food to which your senses awake.

Benjamin Catt (16)
King Edward VI College, Stourbridge

The Taste Of Mexico

Red, yellow, green
Peppers of the regional fiestas,
The hot colour of intense red
Spiced up the volcano.

Salsa spilt on the floor
Reminded me of the Grijalva River.

The hot spices of Mexico travelled,
Texas was my new home
With sizzling dishes of the past.

Fajita
Named after skirt steak cowhands . . .
Roasted on a dancing fire
Burning my tongue.

Natasha Hussain (16)
King Edward VI College, Stourbridge

Best Friends

Best friends are always there for you.
They always say nice things to you.
Friends stay together all the time.
Wherever you go, wherever you play,
They'll always be there to stay.
When you're lonely and need a friend,
You will have a friend to lend.
Best friends are loving and caring.
They can't stop sharing.
When you need a shoulder to cry on,
They will never be gone.
So best friends are like part of your family,
They're there every step of the way.

Aneela Aziz (12)
Lordswood Girls' School, Birmingham

Fox And The Crow

(Inspired by 'The Fox and the Crow', one of Aesop's Fables)

There was a fox who saw a crow,
That had a chunk of cheese.
'You have a beautiful voice, you know!'
Commented the fox with a sudden freeze.

'Do you really think so?'
Replied the crow with a crooked voice.
I think that's a no!
Thought the fox, surrounded by noise.

The crow began to sing,
And the cheese dropped out of his mouth.
The fox caught it in a ring,
He then ran through the forest north then south.

Samiye Mazlum (11)
Lordswood Girls' School, Birmingham

Spring

It came in like a lion
And went out like a lamb.
It came prancing towards us,
And went skipping away.
A mystical thing in the atmosphere above,
Blooming beauty around us and waving a wand.

It came in like a lion,
And went out like a lamb.
No shame did it bear,
As it swept through the land,
Leaving behind a trail of wonder,
Never stopping to stand neither to ponder!

Rosie Stokes-Chaplin (11)
Lordswood Girls' School, Birmingham

Racism

We are the people who suffer
Life just gets tougher and harder
We are the victims of this crime
They've gone too far and stepped out of line
Racism is a lack of knowledge
They have even vandalised our courage
All they do is discriminate
And their hearts are full of hate
Every time I walk down the lane
All I get is grief and pain
My world is falling apart
These people have a stone heart
My life is not worth living anymore
Now I can't even knock on a door
All these thoughts in my head
Now I wish I were dead.

Samera Shane (15)
Lordswood Girls' School, Birmingham

A Tear Of Life

A tear is born in your eyes,
Lives down your cheek
And dies on your lips.

Life,
May only be, or seem to be
A split second,

Like a tear
Comes unexpectedly,
Dies unknowingly.

Sabrina Samra (12)
Lordswood Girls' School, Birmingham

Who Am I?

Who am I inside?
Do I really know?
Do I truly know myself?
Will I ever find out?
I do know my friends
My family
My name
I do know my hair colour
My eye colour
My height
I do know my hobbies
What I like
And dislike
But do I have a soul?
A place to go when I'm dead?
How long will I be alive?
Will I live on after I'm dead?
I don't know my future
What I will do when I get older
Or even if I will live for very much longer
I do have a loving family
And very kind friends
But do they really know me and understand me?
Do I really know and understand myself?
Who am I deep down?
Will I find out in the end?

Roma Palmer (12)
Lordswood Girls' School, Birmingham

Who I Am

I am like my mother.
I am like my father.
I am their child.
But I am not a child, I am a woman.

I follow my heart.
I follow my soul.
I follow my mind.
I follow them all.

I am a child from God.
I am a child from Jesus
I am their child.
But I am not a child, I'm a woman.

I move to the beat of the moon.
I move to the rhythm of the stars.
I move to the voice of my mind.
I move to the sound of my heart.

I am part of a woman.
I am part of a man.
I am a child.
But I see myself as a woman.
Who am I?

Nicole Herbert (15)
Lordswood Girls' School, Birmingham

The First Snowflake

The snowflake falls from a darkened sky
A sight I couldn't tear my eyes away
A downy feather from so high
The snowflake falls from a darkened sky
More snowflakes join in, they dance as they fly
'Please let it settle,' I pray
The snowflake falls from a darkened sky
A sight I couldn't tear my eyes away.

Lauren Wilson (12)
Loughborough High School, Burton Walks

Summer

I sit by the window,
The sun shining bright.
Shadows dance across the floor
As my fingers touch the light.

The curtains billow
And flutter in the breeze.
The faint whisper of the wind
Rustles through the trees.

The sweet smell of pollen
Suffocating the air,
The parched brown lawns,
Stripped of their colour, bare.

The melodious chant of birds
Breaks the scurried rush
Of the soft murmuring insects,
Invading the gentle hush.

A dry, humid mist
Beckons the dusk.
The bright sky fading,
The day has been brusque.

And the darkness comes
Pushing day into night.
The shadows now at rest
No longer dance in the light.

The summer with its cheerfulness,
Wilting, fleeting fast.
My life, like a season,
Fades into the past.

Sarah Louise Oatley (17)
Loughborough High School, Burton Walks

Best Friends

I am fat
You are thin
I like to eat a lot
You like a salad
I joined all the sports clubs
You joined chess
I like to be with lots of friends
You like to spend time alone
I am tall
You are short
My hair is black
Your hair is blonde
But apart we would be nothing
Because we are best of friends!

Zoe Burdon (11)
Loughborough High School, Burton Walks

Why Me?

The lights are flashing,
The heating's off,
I'm sitting here shivering,
I start to cough.

My friends now enemies,
Why me?
I'm feeling empty,
Why me?

The window breaks,
The leaves fly in,
Is this the life,
I chose to live in?

I'm so confused,
I just don't see
Why God, why?
Why me?

Rebecca McChrystal (12)
Loughborough High School, Burton Walks

Snow

I fall from the clouds
Which are loaded and heavy
Delicate flakes which are very deceptive
I swirl and twirl as I fall to the Earth
Like a dancer with a white skirt of lace

The children look up with anticipation
Happy faces full of joy
Down, down I drift with renewed force
Covering the Earth and the snowdrops named for me

Deeper and deeper as I settle and drift
Deeper in the ditches and gullies
Drifting on the hillsides in the wind
In the town and cities traffic moves slowly
As I fall from above to blanket the Earth

Children love me and hope I will stay
Adults hate me and can't wait for me to go
I am *snow!*

Sarina Jassal (12)
Loughborough High School, Burton Walks

Feathers

Floating softly along,
White and beautiful,
Sound and peaceful.
What angel could have sent this beauty?

My mind drifts along with you
As you gently fall.
So soft,
If only everything were like you.

So white,
So pure,
Just like snow;
The beautiful feather.

Coral Andrews (12)
Loughborough High School, Burton Walks

King Of The School

One day at school
I decided to rule,
So I came in wearing a crown.
When teacher saw it
She went into orbit
And then with a bump she came down.

As teacher came down
Her face bearing a frown
I placed the crown, points up on her chair
I took to the hoof
As she went through the roof
And then rocketed up in the air.

Teacher made her descent
Yelled, 'Come back and repent!'
I rushed out of the horrible school
Some people cheered
As others all jeered
And I shouted, 'You know I still rule!'

Elizabeth Cooper (12)
Loughborough High School, Burton Walks

A Random Poem

(This is whatever I'm thinking of)

Valentine's Day sucks,
No matter how hard I try,
I never get praise for my work.
My rabbit hates me,
The dog stinks,
I can't get rid of my spots,
Although they have got better.
I have a zillion best friends,
(Don't ask me to count them!)
I need to be taught how to
Straighten my hair.
I'm feeling depressed.

Fiona Stephens (12)
Loughborough High School, Burton Walks

A Prisoner In A Small Glass Tank

Trapped in a tank,
Where the walls are glass,
No freedom, no life that will last.
No independent life of adventure or glee,
But a prisoner in a small glass tank.

Trapped in a tank,
Where the food is not fresh,
No excitement, no friends - all alone.
No joy of life; just boredom and such,
As a prisoner in a small glass tank.

Trapped in a tank,
Where the water is clean,
No chance of being eaten for tea.
No disease, no problems, no need to work for food, but still . . .
A prisoner in a small glass tank.

Sophie Stevens (11)
Loughborough High School, Burton Walks

Mirror/Rorrim

I have a twin	niwt a evah I
that lives in a	a ni sevil that
mirror and she	ehs dna rorrim
does whatever	revetahw seod
I do. She sees	sees ehS .od I
whatever I	I revetahw
see. I leave	evael I .ees
and she does	seod ehs dna
too. But she's	s'ehs tuB .oot
trapped in a	a ni deppart
mirror and I	I dna rorrim
can't get her	reh teg t'nac
out. So maybe	ebyam oS .tuo
we won't ever	reve t'now ew
meet . . .	. . . teem.

Helena Smith (12)
Loughborough High School, Burton Walks

That Girl

She sits on a park bench, alone in the rain,
She hopes that somebody will notice her pain.
Every day she sees him, standing over there,
The one laughing with his friends, the one that doesn't care.
She thinks she's not good enough, she thinks she's to blame
And he just walks on by that girl, the one that has no name.

So it may seem like she has no face,
Just an unimportant waste of some empty space,
But inside she has feelings and a desperate hope,
She prays that she'll be able to cope
With being invisible, though she's longing for fame
Because he'll just walk on by that girl, the one that has no name.

Now she starts to walk home, alone once again,
She's crying helpless tears though she's nothing to gain,
Don't look at her as though she has no pride,
Start to get to know the soul that must exist inside,
And although you think she's worthless, don't treat her the same,
And please don't walk on by that girl, the one that has no name.

Emma Harker (13)
Loughborough High School, Burton Walks

A Poem For Valentine's Day

When I feel blue,
I think of you,
And everything's OK,
And my troubles don't exist,
When you walk my way.
You have shown in many ways
That you are good and true,
No matter what the rest may say,
I depend on you!

Isobel Jane Fyson (11)
Loughborough High School, Burton Walks

Hope

I lay there, helpless.
The blank walls closing on my small bed;
I took in the clean smell of the hospital and closed my eyes.

Was this the end for me?
I had a husband and a beautiful three-year-old daughter,
Why was God doing this to me?

I had only found out about my breast cancer six months back,
Since then I have been through only pain and agony.
I tried going through it but felt it was time to give up.
Was this the wrong decision?

Was I really going to leave, but where would I go?
Heaven, Hell, or would I rot away underground?
So many questions but I had very few answers.

All I could do was hope, hope for a chance to push my daughter
on a swing,
Hope to grow old with my husband.
Hope for me, and my life which was not yet complete.

Shreenal Ghelani (12)
Loughborough High School, Burton Walks

Dolphins

A dolphin jumps out of the sea,
It pauses - takes a look at me.
I stare and look into its eyes,
This moment I will memorise.

It dives back in and splashes us,
But with this comes a water gush,
And this, I will never forget,
Now it has gone, I feel upset.

Saskia Proffitt (11)
Loughborough High School, Burton Walks

Differences

You may be big,
You may be small,
You may be short,
You may be tall,
You may be f a t
You may be thin
But we are all the same within.

We may be cute!
We may be f i e r c e!
We may have a smile,
We may have many tears,
We may be sweaty,
We may be clean,
But all of us within aren't mean.

I may be different but who cares?
Not me and you shouldn't either!
Because we are all different, every human being!

Eli Taylor (12)
Loughborough High School, Burton Walks

Weekend

It's Friday afternoon,
As we wait in suspense,
We sit on the end of our chairs,
As the caretaker opens the fence.

I'm looking at the clock,
It's twenty-nine past three,
My classmates wait for the bell to go,
And that includes me!

The bell has gone,
And we all say, 'Hooray!'
Now it's the weekend,
We can all go and play.

Uzochukwunasom Oforka (11)
Loughborough High School, Burton Walks

Nature

I see the birds in the treetops,
Chirping and singing a beautiful song,
I see the flowers growing,
Smelling like honey, so sweet and so long.

I see the apples growing
As I taste the gorgeous smell,
I see the bees buzzing,
A few running to a nearby well

I see the sun setting
Going off to bed,
I see the night sky coming
And suddenly the sun is dead!

I see the beautiful animals,
I love everything I see,
I wish I could be here forever,
This place means everything to me.

Saira Badiani (12)
Loughborough High School, Burton Walks

Colours

Red is for roses given for love
Blue is for skies way up above
White is for snowflakes drifting down slowly
Black is for sadness and feeling lonely
Pink is for flowers on little girls' dresses
Green is for bushes, trees and grasses
Grey is for clouds full up with rain
Brown is for a lion's big bushy mane
Yellow is for streetlights shining so bright
Purple is for star-studded velvet nights
Cream is for ponies' fluffy fur
Orange is for autumn leaves that were
Silver is for the moon, a long time gone
Gold is for the sun shining on, on and on.

Charlotte Taylor (12)
Loughborough High School, Burton Walks

The Wind

The leaves are rustling
The wind is whispering through them.
A soft breeze is blowing
Each blade of grass is swaying in time to the wind.

A little sapling is bent in half
Crippled by the gale.
Umbrellas are blown inside out
You can hear the wind howling all through the house.

On the horizon you can see a funnel
Of a dark whirling mass of wind
Black clouds lie oppressively thick
The tornado is coming - wreaking devastation in its path.

But soon the world is calm again
And people like you and me,
Are getting back to their everyday lives again
The wind and the world are at peace.

The leaves are rustling
The wind is whispering through them.
A soft breeze is blowing
Each blade of grass is swaying in time to the wind.

Veronica Heney (11)
Loughborough High School, Burton Walks

Lasting Petal

One lasting petal yet to fall,
Upon a rose standing tall,
Its long straight stem climbs the wall
Holding tight as not to fall,
But that petal has to go,
And like a drop of blood descends to the ground,
Spinning slowly round and round.
And there lies that last petal.

Hayley Evans (11)
Mount Grace High School, Hinckley

My Most Hated Teacher

She's a little gremlin
With hair like dark black horns,
Or maybe she's a werewolf
Turning evil only at dawn.

She's like an age-old vampire
Hungry for my blood,
If only she was calm
Like a springtime bud.

But alas it cannot happen
For she is like a demon,
She can make you so annoyed
It even gets her steaming.

She's my most hated teacher
No doubt, I hate her the most,
Sometimes I wish I could teach her
How to be a ghost!

Daniel Bailey (13)
Mount Grace High School, Hinckley

Life

Life, you think, is in excess,
But that really isn't true,
It could end in three seconds,
And the last thing that you see might be blue.

An army marching towards you,
And you are all alone,
No weapons to defend you,
So you know you're going down.

We are the people who fight for our existence,
We don't claim to be perfect but we are free,
We dream our dreams alone with no resistance,
Fading like the stars we wish to be.

Matt Kiteley (14)
Mount Grace High School, Hinckley

Born A Jew

Just ordinary people
Living an ordinary life,
Grandparents, children
Husband and wife.

The Arian race
No room for a Jew,
To think that these people
Were God's chosen few.

A star on a badge
Picked them out from the rest,
Living in fear
Each day a test.

Trains filled with people
Full of despair,
A journey to nowhere
Does anyone care?

The labour camps beckon
Each one full of gloom,
Spirits are broken
Inside every room.

Stripped bare for a shower
Inside, hear a cry,
With the last of their dignity
They lay down to die.

Hannah Godrich (13)
Mount Grace High School, Hinckley

Valentine

Well here we are again, gotten round full circle.
You tell me you love me, then you hate me.
Why is this so difficult when you know we should be together?
I mean we started off really lovely, telling each other, 'I love you,'
Every waking minute together, hugging, kissing
And lovely things but then again *she* came in.
We get further and further apart
Until you tell me that we can still be friends.
Hah! Men, you're all the same.
So I sit here in my little haven,
You want to come back but I won't let you in.
You've just broken *her* heart but mine has had time to heal,
And now I can tell you that you never will get back in.
And that is the only thing I have learnt from you.
As they say, *sticks and stones may break my bones,*
But the words you said will always hurt me,
So I won't let you in!

Anna Robinson (14)
Mount Grace High School, Hinckley

Frankie

When she's sad,
I'm sad
When she cries
I cry
When she weeps
I weep
When she can't take it anymore
She grabs a knife from the kitchen drawer . . .

Conor Cantle (14)
Mount Grace High School, Hinckley

Grim Reaper's Ghosts

The floorboards creak
The children shriek.

When the kids are alone
The ghosts start to roam.

Hide under your sheet
Feel the racing heartbeat.

As lights go out
The ghosts prowl about.

They leap into fright
So you flick out the light.

They're the reason you're scared of the dark
With their scythes they leave a deadly mark . . .

You wake up and you're shaking with fear
You need to remember they're always near . . . !

Chris Fillingham (12)
Orchard School, Retford

Dogs

(Based on 'Cats' by Eleanor Farjeon)

Dogs sleep
Anywhere
Any bed
Any chair
On the floor
Beside the door
On the rug
All warm and snug
By the fire
A dog's *desire!*
That's proved dogs sleep
Anywhere!

Daniel Clark (12)
Orchard School, Retford

Dogs

(Based on 'Cats' by Eleanor Farjeon)

Dogs chew
anything,
any sofa,
any pin,
every pen,
cupboard door,
now and then,
rug from the floor,
piece of cloth,
wing of moth,
scraps of paper,
one little caper,
wood from a wall,
my new plastic ball,
because - dogs chew
everything!

Colby Siva-Andrews (12)
Orchard School, Retford

Clouds

Clouds are big
Maybe small
Clouds are fat
And sometimes tall.
Shapes can be any size,
Scary faces in the skies.

Dogs or cats,
Clowns in hats
And lots of other things.

Always looking in the sky,
Changing shapes as they fly,
Puffy and fluffy, billowing by,
I'm always looking, I wonder why?

Saskia Wilkinson
Orchard School, Retford

Cars

(Based on 'City Jungle' by Pie Corbett)

It's a farce
having cars,
with all the fuss
for us
of washing
and cleaning,
of drying
and polishing,
of filling
with petrol.
And spraying
and oiling
and waxing too.
Soap is used
to clean the rims
and outer brakes.
The hoods,
the tyres,
the windows
and exhausts
all need a clean as well.
The paint
starts to flake
and needs
repainting!

Nicky de Vries
Orchard School, Retford

Exam Results

Exam results
Feeling sick
In case I fail.

Losing friends
But making sure
We'll keep in touch forever.

Heart stops
Nerves come in
All will be fine
I hope!

Getting an A
Getting a B
Getting a C
What will it be?

I don't know
I only hope
It is what I want.

My legs are shaking
My hair is on end
Envelope in my hand
Shaky fingers
Slowly opening
Unfolding the letter.

I've passed!

Jack Stennett (11)
Orchard School, Retford

Home Alone

When the lights are off
And you're in your bed
Voices start whispering
Through your head,

Tapping at the windows
Knocking at the door,
And, let's not forget,
The creaking floor.

Toys turn to evil,
My tummy goes tight.
This is going to be
An endless night.

Feeling rather sick,
Feeling kind of sad,
Feeling very frightened,
Feeling really bad.

Ghosts are coming to get me,
They're coming from the door,
They're going to come and drag me
Across the bedroom floor.

Turn on the lights,
Turn on the telly,
Lock all the doors;
My legs turn to jelly.

Mum and Dad come home.
They ask, 'How have you been?'
I tell them I was fine
As if I'd never seen
The ghosts and evil toys.
They're even worse than horrid boys!

Phoebe Young (12)
Orchard School, Retford

Sandwiches

Brown bread, white bread.
Round bread, square bread.
Butter, marg or mayo.
Make the outer wrapping
For my favourite sandwich.

Now to choose a filling,
Cheese and onion, ketchup and chips.
Chicken and sweetcorn, carrot sticks.
Chocolate spread and strawberry jam.
Put the lid on and press down firm.

Cut in half across the middle.
Gingerly lift with both my hands
Towards the mouth, open wide
And clamp down fast to take a bite.

Out shoots the onion, chips fly forth.
Ketchup squidges down onto the floor.
Sweetcorn, peppers the table top.
Chocolate oozes in-between my fingers
And the jam surrounds my mouth
Like the leftovers from a vampire's last meal!

Jake Hall
Orchard School, Retford

Thoughts Of A Poem

Things to think, what to write?
   Looking at everything in my sight.
      Thoughts running through my head!
        Cheese, butter, milk and bread.
     What to do? What to think?
   What words rhyme and what words link?
Bees' knees, trees and leaves.
     They all rhyme, I could use these?
       I even have to choose a theme.
         In my imagination in my dream!

Georgia King (11)
Orchard School, Retford

Weird, Isn't It?

A horse was on a mobile phone
He had a bit of a tone!
I heard him say, 'Get me my lawyer'
But the call cut off in the hotel foyer.

Meanwhile, across in the church
A dog was proposing
Using a parrot perch
He said, 'Hey baby, be my wife.'
'No way, you're a lurch!'
And cut him with a knife.

At the Great Barrier Reef
Was a great white shark
With a mouth full of big white teeth
I grabbed my phone and sent him a text,
Yo m8 wich wanna thm surfers u gonna eat next?

James Hislop (12)
Orchard School, Retford

Months

January brings the new year,
February brings some of the snow.

March brings all the wind,
April brings all the fools.

May brings May Day,
June brings the warmth.

July brings holidays,
August brings the hay.

September brings the start of school,
October brings the wind, so cool.

November brings the cold and fog out,
December brings Christmas, oh yeah!

Ryan Lancaster (11)
Orchard School, Retford

Nightmare

When you are home
Your parents are out
You are alone
You begin to doubt.

The floorboards are creaking
The ceiling is leaking
In this old house
The ghosts are creeping.

You turn on music
You block it out
The voices, the noise
The endless night.

The music stops
The silence screams
The worst nightmare
Of all your dreams!

Katie Ray (11)
Orchard School, Retford

Shopping!

Shopping is great!
Money in my pocket,
Shops lie ahead of me;
Trying on new clothes,
Buying tops and shoes,
Lots of bright colours,
Bright pink, bright yellow!
Walking around for hours,
Never getting tired,
All I think about is . . .
Spend! Spend! Spend!

Georgina Tuck (11)
Orchard School, Retford

The Show

Waking up that morning,
Just as day was dawning.
Worrying about today,
Home: that's where I wanted to stay!

The day went fast,
The last hour came.
The only hour,
My hour of fame.

I stepped on stage,
Heart beating fast.
Footsteps behind me -
The rest of the cast.

The curtains went up,
The audience started to cheer,
Clap, clap, clapping,
That was all I could hear!

Waking up that morning,
Just as day was dawning.
Worried for no reason,
Now, I can get on with the rest of the season!

Abi Follows
Orchard School, Retford

An Argument

She shouts at me
I say I'm sorry

She grounds me
I beg her not to

She calls me names
I try not to cry

She punishes me
I don't see why.

Nicole Gregory
Orchard School, Retford

Home Alone

My mum leaves me at home,
I get scared because I'm alone.

We have three dolls with ugly faces,
I think my room is scary,
But there are scarier places.

I lie in the dark in front of the telly,
Dreaming happily, eating jelly.

Then I stare at the screen,
Wow! Those monsters are mean!

All of a sudden the door *dings,*
And at the same time the phone rings.

I answer the phone trembling with fear,
I hear someone mumbling, very unclear.

The woman at the door shouts my name,
I answer but looking out from the windowpane.

I didn't realise it was my mum,
And at that time I fell on my bum.

Emily Gill (12)
Orchard School, Retford

Snow

The snow was tumbling down,
Onto the trees,
And lying thickly on the ground.

Waking up to the cold morning,
Wanting it to be the weekend,
Watching TV for the weather warning.

Getting hats and scarves out,
Wrapping up warm,
As we run out and shout.

Laura Edson (11)
Orchard School, Retford

Food And Drink

Food is great!
Food is fun!
All for your tummy -
Yum, yum, yum!

Have you tasted the new Coke?
You know, an advert with that bloke?
I remember my birthday cake -
The one my brother tried to take.

Drink is great!
Drink is fun!
All for your tummy -
Yum, yum, yum!

Oh, how I love my lemonade,
I drank that and went and played.
When I heard of 'new chocolate'
I had to go and buy the lot!

Food is great!
Drink is fun!
All for your tummy -

Yum, yum, yum!

Amelia Tindall (12)
Orchard School, Retford

Everybody Loves Babies

Why does everybody love babies?
All they ever do is cry!
Now that there's a new one on the scene,
Mum and Dad just shout or say, 'Goodbye.'
Nana and Gramps once asked me,
'Why are you acting so strange?'
You see -
It's because everybody loves babies,
And nobody loves me!

Kerry Morris (12)
Orchard School, Retford

I

From
a mountain
high - I might
fall off and die.
So I from a mountain
high can just fly away.
So I from a mountain high -
It's time for me to say goodbye.

George Webster-Bourke
Orchard School, Retford

Vampires

They come out at the stroke of midnight
Dracula, the leader of them all
From the graveyard to the town
Passing from wall to wall!

He picks his helpless prey
From creeping all night around
He sinks his fangs in his victim's neck
Then another vampire has been found.

Creeping back to his coffin
When he hears Dracula call
Flying with the spooky bats
Over buildings and the mall.

So keep away from vampires
Don't go in their sight
So everyone be aware
They will come again
Tonight!

Jade Miller (11)
Parkside Community School, Chesterfield

Animal Noises

By the lapping stream,
There's a group of quacking ducks,
Overhead a bird goes *whoosh!*
Another is cawing from a tree,
The birds are scared away by a loud snort,
A pig in the field trots back into his sty
'Woof, woof, woof!' a dog barks from the next field,
As he rounds up sheep,
'Baa,' the sheep cry, 'baa, baa.'
A mouse re-enters his hole as the sheep go running by,
'Squeak,' the mouse says and hides further down.

Laura Watkin (11)
Parkside Community School, Chesterfield

Vampire

As the vampire came from the dark
I began to notice its bad bark.
As it got closer my heart began to pound
So I began to run round and round.
Then it bit me in the neck
And I was transformed in a sec.
I just turned and walked away,
Ready to kill another day!

Shane Walker (11)
Parkside Community School, Chesterfield

Pop Singer

There was a pop singer called Ben
Who sang through the top of his head
It came as a blow
When the notes were too low
So he sang through his toes instead.

Adrian Britland (12)
Parkside Community School, Chesterfield

Dracula!

From his coffin he rises,
Into the dark night,
People are his prizes,
He hates the sunlight.

His mission is
To bite,
It's called the 'death kiss',
Unless someone puts up a fight.

He sees some glass on the floor,
But he has no reflection,
He walks through the door,
Into the next section.

In the dark sky,
It is covered with bats,
He's always cautious that morning is nigh,
He hears the scuttling of rats.

His skin is pale,
He draws his fangs,
He doesn't like to fail,
There are lots of vampire gangs.

He draws the blood,
He sees the cross,
Where his victim stood,
Dracula is still the boss!

Anne Marshall (11)
Parkside Community School, Chesterfield

Snow Poem

Sky is white, snow is glistening
Fragile snow flutters and glides
Silent snow sways and swirls
Sparkling snow settles on the Earth.

Katie Digby (11)
Parkside Community School, Chesterfield

The Sound Of Football

The *creak* of the turnstile,
The *squeak* of the seats,
The *whistle* of speakers
Before the team is announced.
The *clack* of the rattle
As it spins round and round.
These are the sounds of my football ground.

The *roar* of the crowd
As both teams come out.
The *peep* of the whistle
As kick-off begins.
Our team's got the ball
We're on the attack
Bang goes the ball, the ace team is back!

Crack goes a tackle
On our ace striker Black,
Now it's a free kick
There's no looking back.
Whoof goes the ball in the roof of the net,
Whoop goes the crowd.
Wish I'd had a bet!

The excitement is building
Bump goes my heart.
Clapping gets louder,
Hurrahs are echoing from stand to stand
The final whistle about to sound.
Yahoo, we did it, we've won the cup
My ears *ring* with cheers as the cup's lifted up.

Alex Wallhead (11)
Parkside Community School, Chesterfield

Recipe For Peace

Blend a slice of friendship,
With just a pinch of love,
Mix a cup of harmony,
With the call of a dove.

Chop up the laughter,
And sprinkle in the smile,
Beat out the evil,
And fry for a while.

Spoon out the suffering,
And throw it all away,
Add in some extra peace,
Simmer for a day.

Bake in the oven,
With a skip and a hop,
Serve on a bed of trust,
A cherry on top.

Christopher Mulliss (15)
Parkside Community School, Chesterfield

America

A mazing beauty that's what she has
M aybe they use Daz
E ating, drinking, having fun
R ush hour starts the busy run
 I n the city people start to hurry
C atching up with a McFlurry
A ll over, people start to relax in front of the TV
with a curry.

Daniel Nowak (11)
Parkside Community School, Chesterfield

Recipe For Peace

Chop a handful of care
Add a drop of laughter
Heat up a chunk of friendship
Add them all to a bucket of love,
Whisk in a sprinkle of trust
Heat everything together again
Which will give you a serving of non-violence,
Finally add a teaspoon of harmony
Serve kindly with charity.

Nicole Milner (15)
Parkside Community School, Chesterfield

Have You Ever Heard . . .

Have you ever heard a sky crying?
Have you ever heard the children sighing?
Have you ever heard the teachers splutter?
Have you ever heard the sun mutter?
Have you ever heard the family moaning?
Have you ever heard your friends groaning?

Stacey Barnett (11)
Parkside Community School, Chesterfield

Orange

An inviting fire
Glowing brightly
A flickering candle flame
A comforting warmth
Or a good feeling
A forthcoming heat
On a fresh summer's morning.

Joseph Bates (11)
Parkside Community School, Chesterfield

The Vampire

The coffin lid creaks open
A fresh victim in sight
And with a flick of his cape
He flies off into the night
Into bat-like form he turns
His face from white to black
No reflection in the window
He knows he'll soon be back
His fangs are pointed, ready
A good angle at where he's stood
He's there ready to bite
He's there hungry for blood
This man, he fears the cross and garlic
It kills him for just one look
For Dracula was born in Whitby
And now he's shut tight, inside a book.

Sarah Raine (12)
Parkside Community School, Chesterfield

Victory

I'm standing impatiently,
I'm waiting for the man in the suit
To blow his whistle,
I keep on thinking and thinking,
I cannot believe I'm competing
For the chance to be number one!

The whistle is blown and now I'm off
Swimming and racing like a scared fish
I'm like a vicious shark that has just smelt fresh blood,
Plunging itself in and out of the salty water,
Determined to catch its prey . . .

At last I am not standing, waiting impatiently,
For I have won the number one title,
I have claimed victory, the *gold medal!*

Simran K Osaan (13)
Rushey Mead School, Leicester

School's Out

The sun outside welcomes me
The clock is slow, as I can see
The teacher drones on and on,
Can't she shut up? I want her gone.

I cannot wait for the familiar ring
Brrrring, brrrring, school's out!

The joy inside me wants to burst out.
Jump up, run around, shout and shout.
I fight the feeling to bounce right up
Drink up the time in a cup.

I cannot wait for the familiar ring,
Brrrring, brrrring, school's out!

The time draws near for me to leave,
It's a time for laughter, not to grieve
I approach the gate with a step across
I hear my name called but I don't give a . . .

I am hearing that familiar ring
Brrrring, brrrring, school's out!

Sudip Chauhan (13)
Rushey Mead School, Leicester

The Last Days Of My Life

Locked up in a dull room,
I can hear nothing but my heart go *boom!*
Desperate to get out and talk to a friend,
Today makes me feel like my life is about to end.
Misery is now a big part of my life,
I might as well end it with the use of a knife.
My life has only used up 13 years,
And the memories bring back icy tears.
Why me God? It's not my fault,
Suddenly my life has come to a halt.
I've also been beaten with a leather rod,
My body is in such pain, I can't even nod.
And there I am lying in an uncomfortable bed,
Thinking about everything going on in my head.
Lonely, isolated, bullied, stressed.
Desperate, annoyed, frustrated and depressed.
Who has the right to do this to me?
I need to show everyone who I can be!

Neha Hathalia (13)
Rushey Mead School, Leicester

Gone . . .

The trigger was pulled,
Time was shot,
He was fading away,
Sweating, very hot,
Which one shall live?
I want the lot,
Everybody has to go,
Every string has a knot.

Hiten Joshi (13)
Rushey Mead School, Leicester

My Letter To Nurse Beauty
(Comic Relief Night, 11th March 2005)

I sit here . . .
                    here in my room . . .
                                        on my sofa
And I watch you,
As you tell everyone that you are dying,
Dying from AIDS.
I look at what you have . . .
And what I have . . .
I feel so fortunate, so lucky to have parents,
Their love and support,
A home,
Food,
Clothes.

I admire your strong will to send a message
Across the world to make a difference,
And your determination
Not to give up and give in.

Shaheena Rajabali (13)
Rushey Mead School, Leicester

Somewhere In The Ocean

Somewhere in the ocean, there is a magic fish.
He made a purple potion and slapped it on a dish.
The potion started bubbling and whizzed up in the air.
The fish then started mumbling, 'There's magic in the air.'

Kiah Howarth (12)
St Philip Howard School, Glossop

Don't!

Don't pick your nose
Cos it makes me mad.
Don't call me names
Cos it makes me sad.
Don't tickle my ribs
Cos it makes me screech.
Don't be mean to animals
Cos it makes me cry.
Don't tell a lie
Cos it makes me annoyed.
Don't blame me
Cos it makes me upset.
Don't disobey my rules
Cos it makes me mad!
Don't do stuff I don't like
And I won't get mad!

Molly Parker (12)
St Philip Howard School, Glossop

The Seaside

The ocean waves lap up against the sand
My dad leads me in holding my hand
It's boiling hot, the sun's so bright
I'm so happy, I'm as high as a kite.

The sand's so hot, it burns my feet
There are plenty of new friends here to meet
The man selling food is very jolly
I think I will have a red ice lolly.

Swimming's my thing, it always has been;
Is that a yellow crab that I've just seen?
The seaside's great, I love it here
I hope we come back again next year.

Lydia Pasiecznik (11)
St Philip Howard School, Glossop

Change

Is my justice done?
Are there enough pains out there?
Is life rotating fast enough?

Or am I to tumble on,
And face this world alone?
Reverberate my thoughts,
How they were so saccharine,
Then a sudden twist,
And a new mask glues on!

Were memories for abusive pleasure,
Or merely for self-righteous satisfaction . . . ?
Were dreams in a wheel of torture,
Spiralling further to my heart
And rendering the soul to pieces . . . ?

Is man the intellect we once thought
Or merely the obnoxious crawler
That revels in indulgence . . . ?

Can we see past our gluttonous ideals
And re-establish our trust
We could provide to others . . . ?

Suk Kwen Leung (16)
St Philip Howard School, Glossop

Flowers

F ragrant in scent
L oving sentiment
O range in colour
W ild orient
E legant petals on a stem that is bent.
R ose that Heaven sent.

Rebecca Fay (13)
St Philip Howard School, Glossop

The Fairy

See the fairy flutter by
See her flying in the sky
Sprinkling magic as she goes
Sparkly wings and pointed toes

In her dress she looks pretty
Oh, what's that? Looks like a kitty
It is trapped up in the tree
'This looks like a job for me,'

Said the fairy as she swooped down
She grabbed the cat, flew to the ground.
In her sparkly, shiny gown
A silver locket was what she found.

She picked it up and inside she saw
A picture of the kitty's paw.
She tied the locket round its neck
And took the pussy to the vet.

Its owner came and took him home
And flew on back to Mr Jones.

Jessica Barnett (13)
St Philip Howard School, Glossop

Sleeping

One stormy night
In the land of darkness
The thunder struck twelve
The clouds covered everywhere
Everything went black
Shadows stilled me.

Joe Wilkinson (11)
St Philip Howard School, Glossop

Dream World

I'm taking a trip,
To where the green grass grows,
And as a slow trickle,
A blue thread flows.
A thread of water,
Very gently trickling,
But trickling nonetheless.
Above birds will be bickering,
And singing sweet, sweet song.
Herons will swoop by,
Preying on poor fish,
With such a watchful eye;
And hawks will glide,
Sweeping up so high.
So beautifully, so gracefully -
Kings of all the sky.

I'm taking a trip,
To where the sun is always shining.
Rain never scrapes the surface
Of the land that I'm describing.
And yet, somehow,
Amazingly,
The grass, the flowers always grow.
As you would see,
If you could (which you can't)
Come into *my* world.
You can't because it's all make-believe
Every single word.
That's right, you see,
It's all in my head,
And it comes to me when I'm fast asleep in bed!

Shannon Gilmore (12)
St Philip Howard School, Glossop

Saviour

Children always look for a saviour
They get smacked for bad behaviour
All they want is a favour . . .
Don't we all?

When you're young, you have a belief
Much to everyone's relief
They don't want it to end in grief . . .
Don't we all?

Don't we all just want a saviour?
Someone who'll grant us a favour?
Someone who'll not hurt us for bad behaviour,
Don't we all?

The cry of a baby
Its parents say maybe
It won't be me . . .
Don't we all?

Sing a sad song
You just hope it won't be long
For Grandpa to pass away
And that's why I say:

Don't we all need a saviour?
Someone who's ready to grant us a favour?
Someone who won't hurt us for bad behaviour,
Don't we all?

Wouldn't it be a relief,
If we found someone in whom we had belief,
We don't want it to end in grief,
Don't we all?

Yes we do,
Yes we do,
Yes, we do!

Chris Page (14)
St Philip Howard School, Glossop

Life

I open the window
Just to hear,
The sound of a bee
Hovering near.

I open the door
Just to find,
Two bottles of milk
Left behind.

I step outside
Just to hear,
The laughter of kids
Next to the pier.

I step back in
Just to find,
The reflection of life
So gentle and kind.

Life should be fun
So they say,
And I enjoy it
Every day.

Kalie-Dee Jones (12)
St Philip Howard School, Glossop

Crumbling Gravestones

Crumbling gravestones
Haggard bones
Mumbling skeletons
Shadows, groans
Glowing, howling
Chill of breath
Terror undead
Stench and dread
After the scream
Numb oblivion.

Amie Murphy (11)
St Philip Howard School, Glossop

Love

Love is an emotion you can't explain,
It sends a tingle to your brain,
Whatever you do in life, love's there,
For, and with, someone to love and care.

Imagine a place, a deserted beach,
Life's trials and thoughts you begin to teach,
Then you realise what love is meant.
To fill up inside till your heart's content.

Someone special, family or friends,
People who drive you round the bend,
People who make you laugh and cry,
People who sit with you watching the world go by.

Love can be of a thing,
A place, a pet or just a sing,
Food, chocolate but school, not
Just all the things we like a lot.

So colour, creed, race or sex,
Whether we speak, email or text,
We all owe a great deal to a
Beautiful thing called 'love'.

Liam Revell (14)
St Philip Howard School, Glossop

Deep Grave

On a dark, stormy night,
I had a great fright,
I was walking through the cemetery with my good friend Jo,
When I felt something grab me from down below,
I looked down to see a worn and torn face,
Grabbing and pulling at my shoelace,
I ran and ran, until I stopped,
Because the cemetery gate was locked!

Fallon Leigh Done (11)
St Philip Howard School, Glossop

Cauldron Of Doom!

Witch's glare,
Wizard's snare,
People beware
Of the cauldron of doom!

Spell 1
Goblin's nails
Slime of snails
Stir this mixture with a chameleon's tail.

Spell 2
Smell of rat,
Claw of bat,
Don't forget whisker from cat.

Spell 3
Frankenstein's blood
Eyeballs with mud
Sprinkled finely over a newly grown bud.

Now you know more of the magical spells,
People beware of the cauldron of doom!

Mark Sierotko (11)
St Philip Howard School, Glossop

Sometimes

Sometimes I'm happy, sometimes I'm sad,
sometimes I'm really naughty, sometimes I'm really bad,
but now I know all the trouble I've caused,
I just wish I had stopped, thought and made a pause.

Louise Farrell (12)
St Philip Howard School, Glossop

One And Only

You were my one and only,
You were my only one.

Then one terrible morning,
I woke up to find you gone.

You'd flown away with the angels,
To the paradise in the sky.

Through those shining Golden Gates,
Up so very high.

There was no one I could turn to,
No shoulder where I could cry.

It was always just you and me,
I never even said goodbye.

I've moved on now, and I realise,
Although I never said goodbye,

I'll see you again when it's my turn to go
To the paradise in the sky.

Faye Allison (12)
St Philip Howard School, Glossop

Four Seasons

The seasons of the year go round,
Like a circle in the ground,
Autumn, winter, summer, spring,
They are all connected in a ring.

There are four seasons to be found,
In autumn, leaves fall to the ground,
In summer and spring there is so much sun,
And winter's the season for everyone.

Hannah Jackson (12)
St Philip Howard School, Glossop

Right And Wrong!

Big, bad, mean
Rude, scrawny, lean
Eyes full of tears
Head full of fears
Bullied!

Help old ladies cross the street
Help butchers, butcher their meat
Pick corn
Mow the lawn
Helpful!

Thump! Slap! Whack!
Don't do it back
It's their loss
Tell the boss
Surviving!

Do what's right
Stop a fight
It's them you must guide
So they be brought by the tide
To the good side
It's life!

To learn what's right and wrong
Doesn't take very long
Just use your heart
Then you're a part
Of guiding!

Megan Fussell (13)
St Philip Howard School, Glossop

The Shandy Latter

Deep down in a lake in Sydney,
There is the most peculiar fish,
One you wouldn't even dream of!
One you would want to miss.

Now, this extraordinary fish,
Goes by the name of Shandy Latter,
It looks a bit like a huge pork pie,
Yes, a pork pie, only flatter.

This fish even has hair!
Its hair's a shocking bright green!
With orange stripes and yellow spots,
And the most colourful nits you've ever seen.

The Shandy has a tattoo on its fin,
In the shape of its favourite teddy,
But beware - don't let the cuteness lure you in
(That's how we lost Uncle Freddy).

And the marvellous thing has a *giant* tail,
Purple, blue and slightly pink,
It's so big it can capsize ships,
It's forced many a one to sink.

But one day, a young fisherman
Stopped to try out his luck
He must have been very lucky indeed,
Because for the Shandy, disaster struck.

That day, the most terrible thing,
Happened to the Shandy Latter,
Now it's in a chip shop,
All covered up in batter!

Caitlin Curtis (12)
St Philip Howard School, Glossop

My One, My Only

I've searched the land
I've searched the seas,
All the hilltops
And valleys.

To find my one
To find my only,
But here I sit
Sad and lonely.

I searched through sun
I searched through rain,
But all these hopes
Ended in vain.

In my hometown
I found you there,
You said you loved me
And would always care.

I found my one
I found my only,
So here I sit
As a family.

Aisling Hanna (13)
St Philip Howard School, Glossop

The Young Policeman

There was a young policeman called Bob,
Who always got hungry on the job,
When it was time for his luncheon,
He nibbled his truncheon,
'Cause he didn't have corn on the cob.

Venetia Wright (11)
St Philip Howard School, Glossop

How Can This Stop?

Blood rushing,
Tension clenching.
Hear screaming,
Hear crying.
People yelping,
But no one is helping.
Something is roaming,
And it is taking.
People are dying,
Why is this happening?
It's breathing,
It's living.
It's cursing,
The potion is working.
More and more are dying,
There is no curing.
People are mourning,
As the day is dawning.
The murderer is rising,
No one is challenging.
The evolution is changing,
Man is weakening, monster is winning.
No one can stop this torturing,
It is meant for killing.

Sarah Wilson (12)
St Philip Howard School, Glossop

The Graveyard

As the ghosts walk through the graveyard
Listen for the howling of the undead.
Look for the glowing of the shadow.
Feel the depth of the oblivious chill.
Haggard bones crumbling away.
Scream, terrified, groan, as the footfalls fade away.

Charlotte Pearson (11)
St Philip Howard School, Glossop

Cornet Girl

Oh well, maybe next time.
I tried my best, fourth place is not too bad
because they were really good players.
I was only three points behind the winner.

Oh well, maybe next time.
Do you realise the girl that won was a grade eight?
I have only just passed my grade five
and I was not far behind.

Oh well, maybe next time.
My daddy thought I was a genius
but they don't appreciate brass players in this world.
My daddy coached and coached but what happened?

Oh well, maybe next time.
My bandmaster goes mad if we make a mistake
but I played my solo perfectly.

Oh well, maybe next time.
My mum thought the young man who came last
was one of the finest players. Oh no!

Oh well, maybe next time.
I am going to practise and practise
and really listen to my music teacher
and then *maybe next time* I will win!

Maria Birnie (12)
St Philip Howard School, Glossop

Artificial Garconade Of The Puppets

Step outside the classroom to hear the monotonal droning,
Of the teenage image propaganda at work.
Move to the rhythm of the tarnished 'What's Hot?' column,
In the latest guide to being acceptable.

Eclipsing himself in hope, remaining in shadow,
There's no way they will find him here,
With his irregular ambitions and no real purpose,
Recoil into inevitable submission.

Examine the prudent atmosphere
And tell me how many souls we've collected,
When an uneducated child is a child lost.
Yet it's all of their own preference.

He won't mirror the reflections of the 'perfect image'.
There's no defending his enigmatic self either,
When it's best to keep quiet and be thought a fool,
Than to open your mouth and remove all doubt.

Move the bishop to B4, evaluate the current situation.
Deceive the opposition, let the pawn ambush royalty.
Perform routine distraction, but the eyes lied deliberately.
They see him, capture him, remove him from the game.

It's beneficial that he found out early,
That after the game,
The king and the pawn go into the same box.

Joan Carr (15)
St Philip Howard School, Glossop

My Dogs

My dogs are really cute
When they going for a walk, the people always toot

My dogs can be a pain
And they love to play games

They always make a mess
Ripping up my dad's vest

They love a swim
They always meet a girl called Kim

After that they go to sleep
Sometimes they weep

And in the morning they always bark
They give my dad a spark!

Eilish O'Loghlen (11)
St Philip Howard School, Glossop

I Like Noise . . .

I like noise . . .
The *thud* of feet on the stairs.
The *slam* of the kitchen door.
The *scrape* of the chair on the floor.
The *whistle* of the kettle.
The *bang* of the cupboard door.
The *rustle* of the packet.
The *swish* of the cereal in the bowl.
The *clank* of the bottle on the table.
The *splash* of the milk in the bowl.
Snap! Crackle! Pop!
I like noise.

David Birch (12)
St Philip Howard School, Glossop

Christmas In No-Man's-Land

These soldiers, sacred ones, their bodies here but their hearts?
At home, Christmas dinner, an empty chair.
Today while a chilling white blanket covers the slain land
Such gentle feathers . . .

Fall in place of Armageddon's hail.
A grey ball - kicked about in Holy Land. Today they play
Yet know it is a lie. A dirty lie. For tomorrow
Their blood shall be spread on the altar of sorrow.

For which dark goddess do we send this sacrifice?
One of life, death and smiles, tears? God's cruel . . . nice?
Their sidelines are a fence of barbed metal and wire
Goalposts are gun turrets that today dare not fire . . .

In this land of make-believe, where the blood ceremony
Has been paused for an interval, God's not bothered,
But a lonely dark angel watches the game. Yes, God is cruel,
Our hearts may find peace, but not in this life's iron rule!

Thomas Rogers (16)
St Philip Howard School, Glossop

The Boy Who Cried 'Maybe'

There was once a boy long ago,
Who always cried, 'Maybe!'
But the peculiar thing was that,
This boy was only three!

If you said, 'Would you like a drink?'
Or, 'Nice weather isn't it today?'
The boy would say, 'Maybe' and then,
Run off to go and play!

His parents couldn't take much more,
They said, 'We'll just be plain.
Do you actually know what 'maybe' means?'
And the boy never said it again!

Emil Tangham (11)
St Philip Howard School, Glossop

The Old Woman

The old woman in the window
A cold white face
Her lonely eyes stare out
Her warm gaze rests on the icy garden
Until the day escapes into night

Marooned by the windowpane
Shut in from the world
Imprisoned in solitude she sits
As the days fade, she remains
As the years pass, she endures

Spring into summer, autumn into winter
Dawn to dusk, she waits
Knowing death will arrive when the snow melts
Held back by frost till her will is broken
Surrendered to time

Recollections still bright, like the light of the sun
Rekindled memories of once being young
Joyous long days full of fun
Where she played happy and carefree with friends
Where have they gone?

The day is now short and turning to grey
She wishes only to go there and play
One last visit which time will deny
In the warmth of the garden
Where her spirit will lie

The day darkens as the sun drops from the sky
Shadows fill the garden, her eyes slowly close
Tired from watching, hoping and despair
She rests, asleep as the first flakes of snow thaw
The sun finally sets on the everlasting day.

Her feet sink into the wet grass
Treading her way down past the trees
The scent of budding blooms envelop her
Feeling the breeze blowing, tugging all her fears away
Her eyes sparkle as she takes in the garden, she smiles . . .

Free!

Jo Nash (14)
Shepshed High School, Loughborough

Human Rights

As I sit in this prison cell
And listen to the morning bell
Tears start to run down my face
Being locked up because of my race

They don't understand, I've done nothing wrong
I get tortured because I don't belong
Life was great until the day they came for me
I wish I could swap bodies, so they, too, can see.

See what we go through every day of our life
To see how we suffer with all of our strife
Every day I find harder to survive
There must be something that keeps me alive

I sit in this prison cell
Thinking that this must be Hell
But I still hope for my days
Where I am happy and no forays

But it's just a dream, one big lie
The only way out would be to die
But when it's dark and I look at the lights,
It makes me wonder, *don't I have human rights?*

Philip Bell-Young (13)
Shepshed High School, Loughborough

Midnight

A ghostly breeze,
Knocking knees,
Someone's outside
There's nowhere to hide.

The door creaks,
The tap leaks,
A falling chair
From downstairs.

Scratching at the kitchen door,
A plate crashes to the floor,
Chilling screams echo through the hall
The bursting of my old football.

Steps on the landing towards my door,
Shadows move across the floor,
In my room a flash of fur
The cat appears with a purr.

Elizabeth Egan (12)
Stafford Grammar School, Stafford

Free Running

Free running is an extreme sport,
Running and jumping and climbing up walls,
Everyone can do it without being taught,
Even if your legs are very short,
Remember you don't need anything with you,
Unless you are doing some jump, completely crazy.
Now it is something you can always do,
Never sit inside feeling really lazy,
I love to do it, I have my own group,
Ned, Sam and I, we love to eat soup,
Go out now and give it a go.

Tom Harris (14)
Stafford Grammar School, Stafford

Temples And Shrines

As I walk through temple and shrine,
I see the statues all so bold,
I don't care about the time,
The buildings are so tall and old.

The buildings are usually red,
They stand tall,
There's a temple dedicated to the dead,
And the monks start when they're small.

The statues are perfected,
The souvenirs are colourful,
The monks are committed,
And the gardens are beautiful.

It is such a nice place,
It is so inspiring,
It makes my heart beat,
But it is so tiring.

Callum Beddoes (12)
Stafford Grammar School, Stafford

On A Dark, Dark Night

Fast, too fast,
On a dark, dark night,
Not a streetlight in sight,
On this dark, dark night.
With a crash and a bang,
An explosion of flames,
The people in the car,
Never to be seen again,
Don't be like this,
Without headlights at night.
Fast, too fast,
On a dark, dark night.

Joanna Craig (12)
Stafford Grammar School, Stafford

My Animal

My animal is a deer,
He can always see fear,
From a million miles away,
Which will help him find his way.

There are animals that care
Who treat others fair
They run from danger
When they see someone like a ranger.

A young deer is called a fawn
They wake from sleep at dawn.
Their fur is spotted with white
So they need to hide at night.

Fawns hide away
Until their mothers come back from catching prey.
They do not fight themselves,
But deep into the meadow they delve.

Samuel White (11)
Stafford Grammar School, Stafford

Pie

Pie is good,
it's made of crud,
and people want to eat it.

Pie is nice,
it's made with rice,
and eaten by people called Gary!

Pie is tasty,
surrounded by pastry,
and will burn your face cos it's hot.

Tim Hawkins (14)
Stafford Grammar School, Stafford

The Bear

Silver moonlight creeps through the leaves,
Highlighting a burly shadow,
Half-hidden by the trees,
Only just awoken, the bear starts to shout,
Stumbling and yelling like a drunken lout,
His strong, wild arms slice through the air,
Like knives, lashing out, paying no care,
His attention captured by an apple core,
The half-eaten packet of crisps proves to be an equally tempting lure.

Seconds later, again on the hunt,
The beast gives a happy grunt,
Bright yellow bins staring at him,
Hypnotising, dragging him in,
Just like a fisherman with a fish.
Like a baby he crawls over cars,
Leaving behind a trail of scars,
Hitting out viciously at anyone near,
Makes the path forward, crystal-clear,
The space behind, laden with bodies of those who got in the way.

While he is sleeping like a log,
Danger is still not far off,
Walk past like a fairy,
Walk past without noise,
If a single twig snaps,
It could break your back,
As this bear's lightning quick reflexes
Will catch you out.

This creature is a fool for food,
Or a man on a mission,
I'll let you decide,
But don't go too near,
Or you'll end up as this bear's dinner!

Rebekah Martin (11)
Stafford Grammar School, Stafford

And Then She Was Gone . . .

There she stood all alone, wondering where it all began,
She had been miserable for years; she knew this day would come,
She looked around for a sign that she could carry on,
She took one step closer and then she was gone . . .

Her life is a sad story, one that I shall tell,
She had never been right since her brother accidentally fell,
Her mum and dad hated each other, and then they started to yell,
That's when she lost her dignity, which she began to sell.

She knew too much which tore her up inside,
Left to defend herself, her sanity began to slide,
In her crummy flat she wanted to hide,
From the people in her life who had deceived and lied.

Her arms were covered in scars and her face stained from the tears,
She had been battling with depression over these past few years.
Instead of having counselling, she drowned her sorrows in beers,
Everyone thought she was heartless, but she still had hopes
and fears.

As she moved closer to the edge and took those last few steps,
She thought about the happy memories, which she had gladly kept,
She looked over her life; full of deceit, hate and theft,
Then she thought of her brother and her heart sadly slept.

So there she stood all alone, wondering where it all began,
She had been miserable for years, she knew this day would come,
She looked around for a sign that she should carry on,
She took that last step and then she was gone . . .

Ashleigh Eden (13)
Stafford Grammar School, Stafford

Future Ambitions

Where will I be in seven years from now?

At Uni,
at work,
or at home killing time?

I will be livin' cheap on bread, milk and beans,
trying to keep out of debt,
whilst still in my teens.

I'll want a car as cheap as poss,
buying it on eBay,
I'll make no loss.

***

I'm now a billionaire just like Bill Gates,
with a Porsche and Ferrari,
to impress my mates.

Don't forget the big house with a colossal pool,
with a Jacuzzi and a hot tub,
now that's kinda cool!

Now that's the end of my future story,
after all I'm only an eleven-year-old kid,
with twenty-two quid!

Joshua Groom (11)
Stafford Grammar School, Stafford

Racism - Haiku

Racism is wrong,
Blacks and whites in unity,
Help 'Comic Relief'!

Adam Cotton (13)
Stafford Grammar School, Stafford

Catch Me As I Fall

Catch me as I fall
Say that it's ended now
Speaking to the atmosphere
No one's here and I fall into nothing
This truth, drives me into madness
I know I can stop the pain if I push it all away

I've tried to kill the pain
But only brought more
A hell of a lot more!
I'm dying, praying, bleeding and screaming
Am I too lost, too lost to be saved?

Don't run away
Don't give in to the pain
Don't try to hide
Though they're screaming your name.

Fallen angels at my feet
Sacred voices at my ear
Death before my eyes
Standing next to me I fear.
Death beckons me, Death will let me within
Upon my end shall I fall in
Forsaking all I've lived for
And rise to meet the end.

Holding my last breath
Safe inside myself
Are all my thoughts of life.
Sweet-raptured light
It ends here tonight.

William Housden (13)
Stafford Grammar School, Stafford

The Netball Parade

Putting the bibs on ready to play,
Playing full games in the middle of May.
Today we played well under the sun
And then at the end, we even won.

> Left and right we twirl and prance.
> Up and down we swirl and dance.

Moaning and groaning their players are mean,
Their teacher is strict, she's a biased machine.
Today we played badly in pouring rain,
Eventually they won, my fingers in pain.

> Left and right, we tumble and fall,
> Up and down, we rumble and crawl.

On Saturday we practise late till four.
I'm sure the next match will be a ball war.
In partners we work on our quick and fast passing
We're ducking and dodging and then we are dashing.

> Oi! Over here, look I'm free
> Look, she's not marking me.

Oh no! The tournament has come round.
No one on the bus is making a sound.
We're all concentrating, thinking hard.
If we don't win, I'll be in a mard.

At the end of the day we came second place,
But we stayed for the trophy just in case!

On the way home we give a great cheer,
But we'll be here again, this time next year.

Danielle Preston (12)
Stafford Grammar School, Stafford

Horses

H olding the reins
O n the pony
R iding through fields
S itting straight and tall
E very Sunday going for lessons
S addle attached, horses are ready

A ctivities, like races
N eighing for their food
D ismounting after a lesson

P lodding behind is Fudge
O r it could be Max
N ot Polly, she's
I n the middle
E questrian sports like polo
S ound very exciting

A lan is the instructor
R uling the ride
E llie is in front

G alloping on the edge of the sea
R olling in their field getting covered in mud
E very horse is shattered
A t 12 o'clock it's all over
T rotting around the arena.

Elspeth Clarke (11)
Stafford Grammar School, Stafford

The Rabbit (Misty)

She sits there waiting
For the stairs to be all clear
She hops one stair
Up, up, up
Then
Down, down, down
She's as fast as an Olympic racer
To run and have her tea
She'll munch and crunch
Till it's all gone
Her strong white teeth are chips of stars
Jet-black eyes, like a piece of coal

She jumps and thumps
Hops and stops
They all have fluffy tails
Cute little arms and legs
She has a home under the ground
And we have ours above

She makes little hops
As babies make little steps
Now that my story is nearly complete
About rabbits
And their habits
I'm sure you might meet.

Emily Harris (11)
Stafford Grammar School, Stafford

The Sloth

The sloth is the laziest of all teenagers,
Some would describe him as a lone ranger.

He flops along with no destination,
Maintaining his levels of procrastination.

Many dislike his bone-idle fashion,
But I adore it with a burning passion.

A monkey friend pops down to ask where he's going,
The sloth is indifferent, as if he's not knowing.

He lives on a branch, which he uses as a sofa,
His other friends think he's a lazy brown loafer.

I treat his stubbornness with utmost respect
Although his life does not hold much prospect.

He lies in a tree which he comes down from rarely,
And that is why I love the sloth so dearly.

Ellis Baker (12)
Stafford Grammar School, Stafford

A Monkey

A monkey, a monkey hangs from the trees
A monkey, a monkey doesn't like fleas
A monkey, our closest relative

A monkey swings on the trees
But we would fall on our knees
A monkey wants a banana
But most of all the manna

When he eats his lunch
He goes *munch, munch,*
With his bunch
Of bananas.

Joe Osborne (12)
Stafford Grammar School, Stafford

The Golden Brumby

Along the mountain tracks
Across the flowing streams,
Came running a golden horse,
Through the bushy-haired trees.

Asking, 'Why? Why? Why did they come?'
Killing, shooting, destroying,
Only one chance to overcome,
Their awful traps of death . . .

'My golden mane flowing in the breeze,
With eyes as bright as the brightest gem,
My head is pounding like a big bass drum,
My worries, the same as any gentle human.

When running I am as fast as any car,
But not for a race but for my worries,
Yet still, 'Why? Why? Why?'
But still running, running, running.

Silver-moon hooves clapping on the rocks,
Golden bamboo with wind flowing through, is my tail,
Muzzle as warm as a summer's day,
My coat is a smooth golden rug.

But still, 'Why? Why? Why?
Asking questions over and over,
In my oblivious head and,
In my fearful, free heart.'

Thomas Henry David Scott (11)
Stafford Grammar School, Stafford

Cat Poem

The rain falls down
Soaking the ground
And glinting in the moonlight
Outside the pub there is a big fight
But a dog has managed to escape from the chaos of the night

The cat prowls along the wall
Always on the look-out
Making sure a dog isn't near
But it's too late, the dog is here

The cat jumps down off the wall
And he bolts for it
The dog chases off after him

The cat scrambles up the tree
Clawing at the bark
The dog, stuck at the bottom
He now begins to bark

The cat is now stuck up a tree
Leaping from branch to branch
But he slips, falling into the darkness
Landing on his feet
His heart, quick on the beat
Quite a daring feat.

Edward Simpkin (11)
Stafford Grammar School, Stafford

Fuzzle

People stroke it, pet it, scratch it, touch it,
Brush it, comb it, bath it, wash it,
They fuss it, play with it, groom it, love it,
This isn't a pet, you tend to forget,
How much you care about your hair!

Jo Preston (14)
Stafford Grammar School, Stafford

The Bat

In the attic of the unwatchful
Old man I live,
Blind like him.

He is slow,
And because of that he is miffed
But I am far more stealthy and swift.

Like a rat,
I have claws,
My ears are big,
And can close doors.

I am a shadow,
When I walk in the night,
He's tucked up in bed,
So tight.

Invisible, I hang down,
Like a woman's gown.
I'm singing for my sight.

With my song I seek my way,
Until the dawning light of day.

William Hammersley (11)
Stafford Grammar School, Stafford

Snow

Snow, diamonds that fall from the sky,
Snow, a frozen drop of water,
Snow, the essential thing for a snowball fight,
Snow, the ingredient for a snowman.

Snow, ideal for sleighing,
Snow, the icing on a house,
Snow, it brings a smile to every child's face,
Snow, amazing!

Jack Hamer (12)
Stafford Grammar School, Stafford

Actions Happen In Seconds, Consequences Last Forever!

Quick! Quick!
No time to lose
Accelerate! Accelerate!
We will never get there at this rate
Faster! Faster!
This light won't wait
Speed! Speed!
That's what we need
Watch out! Wait!
Turn at that gate
Slow! Slow!
Crunch! Bang!
We hit that gang!

Those actions happened so fast
But those moments never last
Now I am sitting here
With a face full of fear
What fate will await?
My destiny is getting near
The police siren
Forever beckoning in my ear!

Alexander John Bradley (14)
Stafford Grammar School, Stafford

The Dove

The dove is a sign of peace,
with no trace of evil nor cruelty.
As he glides through the open air
he spreads his wings, guarding the Earth
like an angel.

The dove is a symbol of love,
its white feathers pure as virgin snow.
The clear blue sky would be a perfect day
for a small, but gentle, bird to fly.

The dove is an elegant feathered friend.
Its beauty natural and flawless,
placid and tranquil,
softly cooing in a light breeze.

The dove is a sign of hope,
the bringer of good news.
Its simple majesty shines
from the heavens, it is filled with peace.

The dove is a sign of new life,
it unites couples in holy matrimony.
And the dove will gracefully fly
up, up and away!

Chris McKay (12)
Stafford Grammar School, Stafford

The Wolf

In a dark and creepy wood
Carefully watching his prey
Ready to pounce at any time
Watching it with his beady eyes
Trying to make no noise
On the leaves crunching under his feet.

Off he goes, pouncing onto his prey
Like a heavy brick
On a concrete floor
Ripping it limb from limb
With the wolf's agile fingers
Nothing left alive in his hands.

Nothing else in the world seems to matter
Concentrating on eating to feed himself
Walking off when finished
Feeling full for the next day.

Emma Landon (12)
Stafford Grammar School, Stafford

Teacher

There was once a lovely teacher,
And a wacky one at that,
Though happy, she was quite a bit fat.
Her smile was huge because of large cheeks,
Her excuse was simple, 'At least I haven't got a beak!'
She had no style,
Because she hadn't shopped in a while,
She had thick black hair,
And her bum was shown bare,
She waddled not knowing what to do,
For some reason she had a thing for glue,
I kept thinking what would happen on the journey,
I couldn't wait to hear her real story.

David Bates (13)
Stafford Grammar School, Stafford

The Train

Rocketing down the everlasting line,
A huge cheetah zooming along,
As fast as a bullet,
As smooth as silk.

Past stations it travels,
Past one hundred country gates,
Past towns and cities,
Past evergreen forests and marine blue lakes.

On and off the people move,
In through doors, the passengers scurry,
Waddling in in a frantic hurry,
They then get off wherever they choose.

The rocket stops and takes a breath,
Then starts its journey all over again,
Down the everlasting line.

Alex Millington (11)
Stafford Grammar School, Stafford

Txtin

T here goes another txt
X xx it had at the end,
T o 1 of my friends
I sent it 2 U from me,
N ow I hope U will TMB

U sent 1 back

L ow battery! Need 2 recharge!
8   pence left, oh no! 2 daddy I go

   Recharged
       Reloaded
           and

Ready 2 go!

Kendall Baker (11)
Stafford Grammar School, Stafford

My Cat

The cat's name is Sabrina,
Sometimes she is vicious,
A lot of the time she is cute,
But she can run like an Olympic runner.

Her fur is soft and cuddly,
Sabrina has black and white fur, she has a pink nose as well,
Cute white bits on the end of her paws,
Her long whiskers are like pieces of wire.

She pounces like a human jumping far,
Sabrina walks in and she sleeps under the breakfast bar,
She sits in front of the fire,
Then she warms up like a pie in the oven.

She eats like a human scoffing his face,
Sabrina drinks like a human licking a cup,
The cat gets sensitive when you are ill,
Sabrina corners people when she gets angry.

She walks elegantly across the drive,
Arches her back when she gets up,
She moves swiftly towards her prey,
The cat moves like a tortoise when she corners her prey.

Sabrina springs like a cheetah running across the desert,
Her fur is as soft as a fur coat,
She sleeps in the house at night and she is up early dawn
to greet 'Hello.'
The cat runs around outside all day, catching prey.

James Cogan (11)
Stafford Grammar School, Stafford

The Weather War

It began as a lovely summer's day,
But then the clouds closed in.
Like advancing armies, they moved across the sky
Then the war cries began and the roar of wind hit the house . . .

Raw power hits the house, I hear it thud
Leaves whip up and hit our windows,
The army is here and they start to fall, hitting the bone-dry ground
Soon the ground surrenders and turns to mush.
But that is not all as the veterans arrive
Taking tiles and branches down and away

Whistling through the garden searching for his prey
The warlord comes whipping around
Taking anything in his way down to the ground
Screaming as he comes, calling for his king
And now the king comes and he comes hard

Hard and fast
Fast as the speed of light
Down come his shock troops
Dropping from the sky taking trees down in a single shot
And the trees burn

The king laughs, enjoying his fun
He laughs, booming away
Loud and deep
Dogs that did bark at the veterans hide and whimper
But the king is tired
And so is the warlord
So they hide away
Ready to rain on another lovely summer's day.

Charles Taylor (13)
Stafford Grammar School, Stafford

A Day At The Seaside

A geing worn-down pebbles lay to rest

D ecorating beaches from tip to toe
A nother sunny day at the seaside
Y oung children play in rock pools

A nnoying, grumpy old women trying to sunbathe
T aking sand near them to build sandcastles

T ogether crowds of people gather in the sea
H owling waves fall and rise instantly
E ffortless waters wander up the beach

S eaweed floats soothingly across the instant ripple
E ventually the sea finds itself coming in
A ggressive winds begin to create spray in faces
S adly the sun is shrinking and fading
I nside, people begin to disappear
D ramatic sunsets appear in an array of colours
E njoying the sunset, spectators watch.

Becky Parkinson (13)
Stafford Grammar School, Stafford

Rain

Rain can be as sharp as needles,
Rain can be as soft as cream,
Rain can be as fast as lightning,
Rain can fall as slow as snow,
Rain can come as suddenly as earthquakes,
Rain can come as slow as the sun,
Ran can be as big as your fist,
Rain can be as small as ants,
Rain can make a beautiful rainbow,
Rain can cause a thundery sky,
I watch it coming,
Every day.
Rain!

Ben Jackson (13)
Stafford Grammar School, Stafford

Young Writers - Great Minds - Inspirations From The Midlands

Tiger

Who is the king
that hunts on the plain
through the flood and the drought
the wind and the rain?

He is the bane
of the exotic deer
he stalks from the side
and strikes from the rear.

With stripes on his side
and pads on his feet
his prowling is silent
his running is fleet.

Who is the hunter?
Tiger's his name,
he is silent and swift
and that is his game.

James Hammersley (13)
Stafford Grammar School, Stafford

Spring

Daffodils swaying in the light chilly breeze,
Lambs play or rest at ease,
Snowdrops and bluebells peep from the ground,
Everyone seems happy all around.

Deep white mist covers the icy cold lakes,
Shh, be careful as the animal wakes,
Pink little buds are starting to bloom,
As the sun rises, there goes the moon.

Bunnies hop and chicks squeak,
Deer and hares run and leap,
Birds, squirrels and badgers too,
As they stroll through the woods, they're watching you.

Chloë McDonald (12)
Stafford Grammar School, Stafford

Football's A Really Great Game

Football's a really great game,
But it can cause you a bit of a pain.
When you burn your mouth on hot coffee,
Just because your team can't win for toffee!

When you miss an open goal,
The manager says, 'You're on the dole.'
Maybe I should be the cleaner
Or a referee like Pierluigi Collina.

One day my club was taken over,
By a Russian called Boris Sharapova.
Maybe I'm a bit of a loony,
But I think our next purchase will be Wayne Rooney.

We were playing Chelsea in the Premiership,
The loser would be relegated to the Championship.
Wayne Rooney penalty, we were up, one-nil!
Jose Mourinho had to take a stress pill.

It ends one-nil, we're staying up,
Next season we're going to win a cup.
Football's a great game,
Let's hope it doesn't cause you any pain!

Scott Goldsbrough (14)
Stafford Grammar School, Stafford

The Poem Of Love

So you meet a girl you love and want to spend every moment
With her.
When you're close to her you feel what she is feeling,
Sometimes you feel trapped and locked into her face and heart,
You don't want to leave her and the moments you have with her.

You dream about her and you want to have her for the rest
Of your life,
It tears you apart, thinking about what it would be like without her,
She was your life, your love, but then you go and lose her,
You don't know what is going to happen next.

Love
That is a big four-letter word
If only we knew what it meant all the time,
The world would be a better place and it would be bound together
If only we could figure it out.

So you go and lose that girl, the one, the only,
How do you cope?
How will you go on?
How will you live?

These are the questions which you must answer

If only she loved me like *I loved her.*

Fiona Brown (13)
Stafford Grammar School, Stafford

Jessie

Jessie, my dog, fluffy and sweet,
greets every dog that she meets.
Puppy-eyed Yorkie, little scraggy tail,
barks every time that you get mail!

Poos on the floor, pees on the rug,
smiles from the top of the stairs.
She always likes a very long hug,
as she scrapes mud on the chairs.

The food that she likes is . . . everything,
especially carrots and chips.
The food that she likes is anything,
except Doritos and dips.

Jessie, my dog, fluffy and sweet,
greets every dog that she meets.

Alicja King (13)
Stafford Grammar School, Stafford

The Countryside

The countryside is graceful.
The countryside is peaceful.
The countryside is quiet.
It has acres upon acres of fresh juicy grass.
The cows graze on the fields, chewing at the cud, as happy as Larry.
The sheep nibble at the newly nourished shoots.
The little birds are tweeting.
The little rabbits are playing in the fresh country air.
The chickens are pecking at insects and scratching the ground.
The little ducks are swimming on the water, ducking and diving.
The farmers are hard at work, ploughing the fields,
Sowing the seed to grow food to feed the family.
The flowers are growing here and there.
All these things make the countryside special in its own way.
So, what would England be like without any countryside?

Lee Swinnerton (14)
Stafford Grammar School, Stafford

The Romany Stranger

The eyes that narrow in the bitter wind,
With the head buried deep in a cloak,
The greyness in the air around,
The ashes and the smoke.

The face that pangs with bitter tears,
And the heart that is still and cold,
The face, spread with a chilling smile,
Hiding secrets that will never be told.

As the dark, thick hair whips the dark, cold skin,
And forward the head tilts slowly,
Ploughing through the mighty wind,
By itself, frightened and lonely.

And as the fog is closing in,
There is a sense of danger,
The figure in the distance
Who is . . .
The solitary, Romany stranger.

Lucy Brands (13)
Stafford Grammar School, Stafford

Views Of Nature

Skipping, running, dancing through the forest,
The babbling brook running beside them,
The moonlight shimmering down on their faces.

The trickle of the brook is calming, honest,
A mouse scuttles into the collapsed den,
Skipping, running, dancing through the forest.

The slow, peaceful dragging of one's young faces,
The grass blowing wistfully in the wind,
Skipping, running, dancing through the forest,
The moonlight shimmering down on their faces.

Emily White (14)
Stafford Grammar School, Stafford

Shopping

So many shops,
So little money,
Pocket money spent,
That's really not funny.

I need a new dress,
I need a new bag,
No, not that one,
It's far too drab!

Gucci, Burberry,
Dolce and Gabbana,
Wrangler and Lee,
Or maybe just Prada.

Embroidered or plain,
Beautiful and bold,
Red and blue,
New or old?

Aislinn George (12)
Stafford Grammar School, Stafford

Tennis

Serve the ball, start a rally,
Play a match, or dilly-dally,
Have some fun, or be serious,
Tennis doesn't make you delirious!

Balls fly at 1-4-7,
Winning Wimbledon is seventh heaven,
Win a set, six to four,
Getting a grand slam doesn't leave you poor!

Become a pro and be the best,
Andre Agassi doesn't wear a vest,
Or Tim Henman for that matter,
Smash a ball and make it splatter!

Nick Baker (11)
Stafford Grammar School, Stafford

A Dragon's Tale

His emerald-green eyes,
Glitter, sinister in the moonlight.
His long golden talons sparkle,
As he sets off into the night.

His webbed wings spread out,
Like a ship setting sail.
His teeth are like ivory,
White, cold and pale.

He swoops down on a village,
And all the people scramble.
He happily chuckles to himself
On his dark midnight ramble.

Golden fire spurts from his nostrils
All the villages gasp,
The church is burning down,
How long will his rampage last?

The churchyard is ash,
The buildings are all charred.
The fiery creature's work is done,
The villagers' minds left scarred.

Daisy Cuffley (12)
Stafford Grammar School, Stafford

Why To Me

Green hills roll away into the distance,
Everything looks so beautiful.
But behind me
I hear cries of war.
Bombs being dropped,
All because two people disagree.
Why is all this happening?
Why to me?

Hayley Tomkinson (14)
Stafford Grammar School, Stafford

The Troublesome Cat

Sharp claws
Deafening roars,
Frightening screams
Deadly dreams,
Someone's there
Waiting to scare.

Open the door
A little bit more,
Stare outside
Nowhere to hide,
Scary shadows
Cast the meadows.

Stand screaming,
Light is beaming,
Watchful eyes
Terrible lies,
Breaking pots
Swinging cots.

Light appears
Life nears,
Sitting staring
Teeth baring,
Sat on the mat
The troublesome cat!

Kate Jupp (13)
Stafford Grammar School, Stafford

Politics

The world has many problems
Many people try to fix
They try to make the right decision
It's a world of politics.

While children die in Africa
Spacemen find a new galaxy
While letting children starve
And wasting valuable money

Black and white
Pick a colour
After all, outside counts
Or does it really matter?

Pay back money
You haven't got
It's impossible
The government have a lot

When we fight in wars
We kill our own species
Fighting nations against nations
And countries against countries

So let the children starve
Judge people by their skin
Make Africa pay back money that's not theirs
And fight other countries' kings.
Or we could do something about it!

Becky Turner (13)
Stafford Grammar School, Stafford

Snow

Kept wandering, alone, by myself,
Watching the snow drift to the ground.
Now the whole world seems to be a white blanket,
You can just hear your heart pound.

Walking at this time,
There's not even a sound.
You could hear a pin drop,
And no one can be found!

The snow keeps on drifting,
Is there no end?
The powder crunches underfoot,
There is no help, no one to send!

This simple event,
Makes my troubles disappear,
It is so peaceful,
There are no problems here!

Dan Smith (13)
Stafford Grammar School, Stafford

The Soldier

There was once a soldier, tall and strong,
Marching in tune with his company, singing a song,
Not making a sound as another foot falls on the floor,
Not making a sound as he slams the door.
All the time his gun in his clenching hand,
The greatest soldier there was in all the land.
Proudly he marches into the fields of death,
Towards the dragon with its fiery breath.
On his chest he wears medals of gold,
Exciting stories to tell as he grows old.
A battle scar is engraved on his face,
One of his injuries he must embrace.
He is like an eagle prowling the skies,
Never giving up as he always tries.

Tom Mawman (12)
Stafford Grammar School, Stafford

Water

Water is the elixir of life,
Without it we would live in strife.
It's a jewel in creation's crown,
This reviving liquid is treasure raining down.

But water comes in many forms,
Rivers, streams, showers and storms.
Rapids, falls, lakes and sea
Monsoons, typhoons and tsunami.

Water drips, trickles and pours,
Moves gently, swiftly, fiercely and roars.
Clear and murky, colours rainbow through,
From turquoise to midnight, all shades of blue.

The feel of water refreshes and cleans
Used to wash, launder, shower and sheen.
It removes the residue of dirt, sweat and tears,
It quenches our thirst with tea, squash and beers.

Without water, life would wither and die,
People suffer now, their crops begin to dry.
Reservoirs and bore holes are what we need,
It will bring harvest, so folk can feed.

William Malpass (14)
Stafford Grammar School, Stafford

The Wind!

This magical whisper takes all that it wants,
It travels across mountains that climb to the sky.
Sometimes it comes to rip up the roots from their home,
Shattering and crumbling the cities of wonder.
It gives no mercy at times of its travels,
Yet at others, it sweeps across your face
Leaving you speechless and dazzled.
This wonderful something spreads the seeds of life,
But don't forget the whirlwind of destruction inside.

Emeline Makin (14)
Stafford Grammar School, Stafford

Independence

One beautiful sunny day,
It was beaming down, so warm
On the field,
And not a cloud in sight -
'Twas so bright
And I dawdled forward,
Looking around,
The grass brushing against my feet.

Spellbound,
In tranquillity I wandered,
And there lay a single,
Solitary dandelion
Before me.

To see such an independent thought,
Growing in the meadow of conformity,
You couldn't help but to lean down,
Take note
And leave with a smile.

Alas, there are very few who would trample
On the small thought of independence.
The independence that gladly tells all:
I am me, and I am willing.

Merlyn Rees (13)
Stafford Grammar School, Stafford

The Grengeler Poem

The Grengeler lives in the darkest of places,
It lives underground, where the sun never faces.
It loves mud, that's one simple fact,
If you ever see it eating mud, you know it's an act.
The home it makes is slimy with goo,
As it cannot eat mud, it cannot chew.
It has to dissolve the surroundings it takes,
With its acidic mucus, its home it makes.

The Grengeler has no legs, it is a slider,
It wishes to evolve, grow legs like a spider.
It's all hairy like a big bear's back,
But one problem, eyes it seems to lack.
Maybe one day its eyes got lost
In its hair, covered like moss.
The colour, its fur is quite crazy!
Don't look for too long, your eyes will go hazy!

The Grengeler is a solitary creature,
That's another interesting feature.
But don't get me wrong, alone it's quite happy,
But sometimes aggravated, it gets quite snappy.
But with what I suppose, it has no teeth,
I guess it's all what lies beneath.

Dan Edensor (14)
Stafford Grammar School, Stafford

Hate Me

You fed me speeches of poison
and made me swallow them whole.
I coughed, spluttered,
Sticky liquid touched upon my lips,
Seeped down my chin
Like a gurgling newborn.

I became scared and hid under your wings,
dusted with filth from your flights
through the night sky.
I questioned your motives -
You took your stick and whipped me,
Lashes across my back.

When I cried you stuffed rags into my mouth,
Prepared, soaked in a vile concoction
of frothing saliva.
I struggled - I wish I hadn't.
The knots upon my wrists became tighter
and my veins became more visible.

I shrieked at my rope burns
into which you poured bleach.
Each time I yelped you kicked at my ankles
so I bled and bled until the scratches became cuts,
the cuts became infected,
the scabs peeled and peeled until they could scab no more.

At dawn each day I would wake up
to see rays of sun shining through the cracked, crumbling bricks,
but then you would return to me and the rain fell.
The rain fell faster and harder and the lightning cracked.
Thunder rumbled, but after a while the sounds of thunder
Merged with the rhythmic banging of my head, against the stone wall.

Jennifer Brown (17)
Stafford Grammar School, Stafford

A Single Tear

I really need to tell the story,
The one that has scarred me inside,
The one that punched me in the stomach
And made me wished I'd died.
The one that stole my childhood
And took away my friends,
The one that brings back memories
Which will taunt me to the end.
The one that took the joy away from the song,
The one that made me realise that I was wrong.
The one that removed the smile from my face,
The one that filled me with sorrow and disgrace.
The one that separated me from all I knew,
The one that divided me from you.
And when I sit in my comfy chair,
And dream of you and your brown wavy hair,
Your beautiful smile that lit up my day,
The feeling I thought had long gone away
But when I left my old school,
I realised that it wouldn't be so cool
To start again
All fresh and new,
And to be so far away from you.
Yes, I've got new friends
But yet inside,
The love I have for you I cannot hide,
So when you see me
On my own, crying a single tear.
You know I'm longing for you
And for you to be near.

Emma Rowbottom (13)
Stafford Grammar School, Stafford

Mistakes

If you could do it all again,
Would you?
And change all those stupid mistakes.

Go all the way back,
Way back to the start
And take all those lucky breaks.

Reshape every moment, rewrite your life,
Get rid of the anger, hate, pain and strife.

Live life to the fullest, like every day is your last.
Live for tomorrow, forget the past.

Face your fears, change your face!
You've time to search, find your place.

Give life a meaning, give love a chance.
Fear no evil. Life enhanced.

Change the world, make a stand,
Your hand's been dealt, so change your hand.

All the answers and all the time,
Change your life if it's not a crime.

But without mistakes, where would we be?
You wouldn't be you, I wouldn't be me.

Change your ways, perfect your life,
I'll keep my anger, hate, pain and strife.

If you could do it all again,
Would you?
I wouldn't.

Alex Roberts (14)
Stafford Grammar School, Stafford

Our Graceful Planet

Our planet is a humble ball,
A dot beside our sun,
But peer closely, there's more,
The works that God has done.

Animals call, insects crawl,
Trees stand tall, then sometimes fall.
Seasons come and seasons go,
Rivers, lakes and oceans flow.

Quakes and quivers shake the land,
Shakes and shivers and lots of sand.
Waves come high at thirty feet!
Sun and snow and sea and sleet.

We have mountains ever so high,
Engulfed in clouds that sometimes cry,
A giant of rock, a being of stone,
Rising above in the shape of a cone.

Forests and deserts sweep the Earth,
To which Mother Nature has given birth,
A million acres of untrodden turf,
A planet with a lot of worth.

And yet amongst us to this day,
There are men that trees they slay,
Forests, birds and creatures die,
As our days go passing by.

We kill animals just for fun,
But what if the tables were suddenly spun,
They'd come up and hunt us down!
Wreck our cities and our towns!

You may be sitting now at ease,
But take this as a warning, please.

David Fallah (12)
Stafford Grammar School, Stafford

Dogs

They're incredibly clever,
They don't mind the weather.
They live in a dog house,
And will *not* catch a mouse!
Dogs love thinking where to pee,
While watching the occasional TV,
Dogs despise cats,
They're even scared of bats,
Dogs would like to sleep indoors,
But the carpet would get dirty from their muddy paws!
Dogs are supposedly colour blind,
But who knows, do they really mind?
Now . . . dogs are a greedy bunch,
They will moan and groan if you fail to give them lunch.
Dogs love their special treats,
Ham, chicken, beef, lamb or other delicious meats,
Dogs are man's best friend and right on top,
They will run and play until the day comes to a stop,
So buy a puppy and your money will buy,
Love and a friend, who cannot lie.

George Mason (12)
Stafford Grammar School, Stafford

Summertime

Summer is the best time of the year,
Until autumn falls,
More kids come out to play
Many get ice creams,
Even though they will soon melt,
Running up and down the streets, getting into trouble.

The sun gets hotter,
In go the kids to put on sun cream,
Many even go on holiday,
Everyone has lots of fun playing in the sea.

Emma Bailey (13)
Stafford Grammar School, Stafford

Homeless

He has nowhere to call his home
He makes his way all alone
Nowhere for shelter, nowhere to stay
Just shop doors and motorways.

He once had money, he lost his bets
He spends what he *doesn't* have on cigarettes
Searching through bins, desperately
Where will his next meal come from?

He always took for granted,
All the things he had.
Now he's been left stranded,
Stranded without a will or way.

He has nowhere to call his home
He makes his way all alone
Nowhere for shelter, nowhere to stay
Just shop doors and motorways.

Paul Greaves (14)
Stafford Grammar School, Stafford

School

School can be good, school can be bad,
But it's always the teachers who make you sad,
So if you go to school and you're feeling down,
Blame it on the teachers if you have a frown.
For they make you miserable and upset and sad,
It is their fault that you're angry or mad.

If you have teachers who are horrible and strict,
They will usually shout at you and beat you with sticks.
They set you hard maths that takes all night long,
Then they say, 'Go away, get out and be gone!'
And you know you will get it all wrong.
Not explaining a thing, you have to leave,
For if you stay longer, they will rant and rave.

Joshua Chick (14)
Stafford Grammar School, Stafford

Don't!

Don't do this!
Don't do that!
That's all I hear.

Don't spit out your dummy!
Don't throw your bottle!
Don't have a tantrum!
That's all I hear.

Don't draw on the walls!
Don't play in the mud!
Don't suck your thumb!
That's all I hear.

Don't bite your nails!
Don't tease your brother!
Don't jump on your bed!
That's all I hear.

Don't answer back!
Don't use that tone with me!
Don't watch TV all night!
Don't play your music too loud!
That's all I hear.

Don't stay out till all hours!
Don't do drugs!
Now . . .
Go live your life.

Dominic Moseley (11)
Stafford Grammar School, Stafford

Mr Bush

Four going on eight years,
A term and a bit gone,
Too much for you Mr Bush?
Lives on your shoulders,
Yet not conscience-stricken.

Your first year in office,
Must have been the best of your life.
How many months was it on holiday?
Then again, a tan and a great swing,
Oh yeah, and that defence report you didn't read.

Biggest attack on your soil ever,
Where were you again?
School! Great! Just where everyone wanted you.
Hope you enjoyed your read,
What was it again? Timmy the Turtle!

The hide and seek in Iraq,
Was there any point?
Did you know you would fail -
Or are you just a bad loser?
Trying to punish the person who had won.

So Mr Bush, four going on eight years,
You've made us aware of many dangers:
Terrorists, the Taliban and American salted pretzels,
We now know who the Pakistani leader is . . .
No wait, we don't!

Thank you Mr Bush!

Ian Watt (14)
Stafford Grammar School, Stafford

The Sail

The sail
where the
wind flies as
I drift through
the water. The
boat keels over as
the wind hits the sails.
The boom skims the water.
I'm not scared. I lean back
coolly, as if it was usual to sit
upright. I see the centre-board
coming up to breathe, it glistens
in the sunlight - a sunbeam dance.
Sparkle, sparkle, shimmer, shimmer.
Suddenly, the wind dies . . . all is still.
The boat now hardly moving is defeated,
dead and still. The sea fog rolls over the hills . . .

Jack Atkinson-Willes (11)
Stafford Grammar School, Stafford

From Deaf To Death

They stand in their smart suits and ties,
With plugs in their ears, they can't hear the cries

Of mothers and children far away,
Who may not live to see another day.

'We care for their country as much as ours.'
As if this country is full of flowers

That dance around all day and night,
The reality is more of a fright.

The flowers here are strewn in a long list
Of death and suffering for those who did exist.

But what do those men think of these fearful flowers?
Why should they care, they have the power.

Ruth Millington (13)
Stafford Grammar School, Stafford

Football

I'm here to be kicked
Right up high
Kick me really hard
So I can fly

Put me on the spot
Give me a whack
Have hope in that shot
Make the keeper stay back

With one great smash
And a lot of power
I went straight into
Your mum's prize sunflower

One week later, punishment done
Out I come
Full of bounce
Ready once more to have some fun!

Philip Spragg (12)
Stafford Grammar School, Stafford

Haggard

To see you again
But not to see you leave
It causes me pain
It feels strange to want to grieve.
I have no tears running down my cheek,
But inside a river runs fast
My happiness has reached its peak.
The only smile I have is remembered in your past,
You look so peaceful, sleeping
Your face deceives us, looking peaceful
Your peers fight hard against our weeping
'Cause your life, hectic, couldn't be dull
But joy comes, I'm glad to have loved you.
Your memories arrive again with each morning's dew.

Michael Yates (15)
Stafford Grammar School, Stafford

The Bundler

Deep in the darkest of forests,
In a small, concealed hole,
Lives a small and secretive bundler,
Tucked away underground like a mole.

He has long bony arms and a rather big nose,
A neck piled with fat and rather big toes.
His body is plump, his head large and round,
He scurries around without making a sound,
He has short stubby legs and padded flat feet,
He creeps around looking for good things to eat.

He scoops up all he finds with his spider-like hands,
So precise, they could pick out just one grain of sand,
His eyes are like marbles, shiny and black,
He carries his grub in a shabby straw sack,
Always alert, avoiding all life,
But for bad situations, he carries a knife.

Although rusty and old it's still very sharp,
And as people will tell you it leaves quite a mark.
When the bundler gets home he feasts on his catch,
He lights up a fire with the strike of a match.
When the day is over he rests his head
On his small fatty neck but he calls it his bed.

Ben Hughes (14)
Stafford Grammar School, Stafford

Young Writers - Great Minds - Inspirations From The Midlands

A Poem About Teachers

Teachers are a funny breed, this advice I hope you read,
Some of them are aliens from outer space; some of them have
A really ugly face,
Long and lanky, short and fat,
Some of them are witches that turn into bats.

After lessons they walk out the door,
While their big bums sag right down to the floor,
If they hear just the slightest noise, they will pause,
And stomp back upstairs, clenching their claws.

They grit their teeth, their faces go red,
As red as my granddad's burned, bald head,
They get out their notepads and write down 12:05,
Looks like I'll be coming back tomorrow lunchtime.

Sitting in detention, biting my nails,
Staring at the teacher who is as fat as two whales.
Being in detention is worse than fine,
I would rather be writing one hundred lines.

After detention they go and have their lunch,
You listen through the staffroom door and all you hear is crunch,
I really, really, really, really, really want to find out
What happens behind . . . the staffroom door!

Hannah Inglis (12)
Stafford Grammar School, Stafford

The Lion King

It's beady black eyes,
Its golden coat,
Its teeth as white as snow,
It runs across the African plain
Roaring as it goes.
Its bright orange mane
Its huge yellow paws,
The king of the jungle roams.
The jungle assemble
To listen to what the Lion King needs to warn.
A fire in the jungle!
What must they do now?
Run, hide or stay there to die?
They must run.
So the Lion King leads the way
Across the plains
To a safe place where they can stay.
The lions, the zebras, the cheetahs go,
The baboons, the birds and the tigers as well
All come together
As one or as two.
Will they be safe?
Can they be sure?
No one will know
And how long for?

Ginny Tallent (13)
Stafford Grammar School, Stafford

Untitled

I hate the Internet
.co.uk
If you can't win,
beat them
I hate full stops.

Laugh in the face of danger
then hide until it goes away,
Don't break the rules,
just cheat!
I hate religion
Amen.
I love stones,
they rock.

Cameras should be round
because they just keep rolling,
I hate poems that rhyme
line
after
line.

Don't write in green,
Don't talk to yourself.
'Who said that?'
Poems should be read,
So why is this in black?

Nicholas Lawrence (14)
Stafford Grammar School, Stafford

Monster Poem

When you are little you're scared of a monster,
a monster under your bed.
You're scared it will eat you,
or worse, it will tickle you.
But is there a monster at all?

Is it just shadows
or little wild mice
that make you afraid when it's dark?

Why are there stories
that make you so scared?
Why can't they all be happy?

When I was little
I knew I was scared
of the monster under the bed.
Or was it just shadows
and little wild mice
that scared me when it was dark?

Sophie Bohanan (13)
Stafford Grammar School, Stafford

Skiing In A Mountain Range

Waking up at dawn
Strap your lead weights onto your feet,
And put on your worthy swords.
A shuttle glides through the mountains to the highest possible reach,
Get off and face your fears.

Standing in the sky,
Surrounded by an ocean of blue,
Cold air rippling through your face,
The wonder of it all, the scenery there to embrace.

Plummeting down the mountain,
Knives slicing in the snow.
Snow so crispy, so powdered
And full of an almighty glow.

Steep, deadly, headlong slopes,
Surround you in wonder,
The air so cold, so spiritless.
Finally you come to a halt,
Strangely, the world slows down.

Jacob Billington (11)
Stafford Grammar School, Stafford

The Beach

The tang of salt fizzing my taste buds,
The soft scrunch of sand beneath my feet.
The calm sea lapping on the shore,
Seagulls squawking as they glide and swoop over me.

Soft sand dunes pierced with sharp marram grass,
Shades of emerald green and sapphire blue
All around me.
Smooth pebbles beneath my toes,
Golden sand like castor sugar sieved
Through my fingers.

Jellyfish and crabs at the water's edge,
Drying out under the midday sun.
The same sun that makes the sea dance
And glitter,
The same sun that warms my back as
I splash contentedly in the shimmering rock pools.

Sam Shaw (14)
Stafford Grammar School, Stafford

Michael

M y monkey's name is Michael,
O n his birthday March the fourth.
N athan bought him a go -
K art, the best present of all.
E veryone had a great time,
Y es, the party was a big success.

M ichael did enjoy it and back
 I nside we played and played and played,
C ome Monday, still we played and played.
H a, ha, a joke book, loads of laughs,
A nd yet another colouring book
E verything was wonderful
L oads of fantastic presents!

James Yeo (12)
Stafford Grammar School, Stafford

The Air Goddess

Elegantly she swoops and glides,
Silently she shows her pride.

High, high up in the skies she's soaring,
She flies and flies and never finds it boring.

Scouring, searching,
For prey that is lurking.

Gliding over mountain tops,
Seeking, searching, she never stops.

She stops and hovers, ready to kill
She plunges to the ground, knowing she will.

This air goddess has killed her prey,
To feed her chicks during the day.

Elegantly she swoops and glides,
Silently she shows her pride.

Rebecca Hawkins (11)
Stafford Grammar School, Stafford

F1 Grand Prix

The sun beats down
The scene was set
The car on the grid snarled and revved.
The drivers were tense, ready to go,
The lights went green and away they blow.
Into the bend they squeal and brake,
Ferrari, Mercedes, Renault.

Schumacher, Button, Montoya, the rest
Like gladiators of old,
Who'll be the best?
Hour after hour they speed around the track,
Fuel, new tyres, must get back.

The race is won, Ferrari of course,
Schumacher the victor on the prancing horse.

William Stuart (14)
Stafford Grammar School, Stafford

Dogs

Shiny wet nose
Rigid back
Very mischievous
Eyes of black

Bottle brush tail
You fly through the grass
Your lovely pricked ears
I look at you, as you pass

I hold your lead
In my hand
I run with you
Across the land

Your tongue hangs out
Like a wet sponge
I throw your stick
And you lunge

Your loud bark
And tail thin
Fetching your red balls
Shiny golden skin.

Nick Bourne (11)
Stafford Grammar School, Stafford

The Forward's Game

Crouch! Hold! Engage!
Three words in control of two huge masses,
Crunch is the sound produced
By a pair of human troops.

Crouch! Hold! Engage!
Watch for the props,
As they'll crop,
All the others,
Resist in vain.

Crouch! Hold! Engage!
Watch for the second rows,
They'll soon flatten your rows,
And upon impact,
You'll have to wish
That you'll survive.

Crouch! Hold! Engage!
Physicality is one thing this is full of,
Girls say 'Ewww! at the sight,
Crack splits your funny bone,
Pointless is the opposition's plight.

Crouch! Hold! Engage!

Srinivas Cheruvu (13)
Stafford Grammar School, Stafford

Helplessness

Terrifying frustration,
Not able to help.
'You're too young!' they say.
No money to pledge.
So much pain, hunger and death,
People not caring,
They think you're mad.

I want to travel, be free like a bird,
Give love and care for people who have none.
Why can't I help?
Why doesn't anyone else?
Too much inconvenience, they don't have time,
I want to take a gap year, visit orphans.
I don't have the money, I have to go to uni.

I want to wipe out suffering all on my own,
I have too high expectations.
I won't cope with the load!
In this modern world, why do people still hurt?
No magic wand to make it disappear,
Why can't we merge, all countries be as one,
To stop the suffering, it's impossible.

Jessica Keitley (14)
Stafford Grammar School, Stafford

Rush Hour (Song Lyrics)

How do you expect things to ever last
When people's lives, they move so fast
Don't worry life won't go sour
If you step out of the rush hour

Life in the fast lane isn't great
You have to mix with people you hate
If you just take one step back
You will see what life can be

Take a breath and look around
Stop and listen for that special sound
You might find what we're looking for
Cash, cars, money and much, much more

How do you expect things to ever last
When people's lives they move so fast
Don't worry, life won't go sour
If you step out of the rush hour.

Nicholas Henderson (15)
Stafford Grammar School, Stafford

Don't Cry

I'll always be here with you in my heart
And I promise we will never come apart
Don't stand by my grave and cry
I will always be here and never really die
I love you and you love me,
That is the best thing life can ever bring to me
A candle will always burn with our flame,
I just wish things could stay the same,
Now I have got to go
With nature's wonderful flow
You will always be my treasure,
Never forgetting, forever and ever.

Shane Cox (13)
The Grange School, Stourbridge

Is It For Real?

Is it for real you're out of my life?
Why did you use that blasted knife?
Even though we're not together
I will think of you forever.
Me and you we never fell out
I know that, without a doubt.
All I want is one last touch
'Cause I loved you so much.
I think of you when I see the moon,
Don't worry I'll be there soon.
Why do people have to die?
When all it does is make us cry.
I cry myself to sleep
My thoughts for you are so very deep.
Is it for real you're out of my life?
Why did you use that blasted knife?

Chloe Salter (13)
The Grange School, Stourbridge

I'm Gone Away Now

I'm gone away now
Never to return.
I do not breathe
I do not hear
The silent cry
Every day and every night
I love you dearly
And will never forget
The happy memories
Which we shared together,
I may not be there in body
But don't forget my spirit,
Will always be with you.
Please don't weep
After all, I'm just asleep.

Ami Bevan (13)
The Grange School, Stourbridge

Young Writers - Great Minds - Inspirations From The Midlands

When The World Turns Its Back

When you look through that window
And walk through that door
You wish to go back
To when you felt something more

As you enter that classroom
And your heart turns to glass
You go numb to those school friends
Who cuss and harass

Sitting down on that stool
Another knife in the back
You try to convince
You don't miss the love you lack

Walking out of that classroom
Gazing at the skies
You know they can't see
The tears in your eyes

So when the world turns its back
And the sun doesn't shine
You then realise that the love
Is the one thing you pine.

Jordanna Holton (13)
The Grange School, Stourbridge

Holidays

I love holidays in every way,
I wish I could go every day.
Spain, France - in a caravan too,
You will have lots of fun at the clubs,
While Dad goes to the pubs.
Mom's sunbathing by the side of the pool,
And the food is so yummy, that you could drool.
We've had a good time, now we go home,
I can't wait for my next holiday - in Rome!

Katie Middleton (13)
The Grange School, Stourbridge

Never Alone

Although you've left,
And now walk above.
I'm never alone
I'm trapped in your love.

I feel you in the morning,
When at first I awake,
Your thoughts are with me
With each decision I make.

I need him to be here
To show me who I am,
To show me where I came from
If he left, part of me would leave
I would be someone different.

Somewhere in my dreams tonight,
I'll see you standing there.
You'll look at me with a smile,
Life isn't always fair.

Tracey Evans (13)
The Grange School, Stourbridge

Don't Go

Now you're gone
You know I won't be able to carry on.
I feel so lost without you near,
I really wish you were still here,
Now you've gone to sleep,
I will really weep,
I will cry every night and day,
Thinking and caring in
Every single way.
I will love you forever,
Even though we are not together.

Kyomi Johnson (13)
The Grange School, Stourbridge

Grief Poem

I will remember you forever and always
As long as I live, till I die
Soon I will be with you in the sky
All I have is pain in my heart
For as I do not want that
I will meet with you again
(Some day some time).

Christopher Perks (12)
The Grange School, Stourbridge

Untitled

My heart is no more
Like an empty floor
Now you are gone
Everyone around me is dying
But I know you are with God
Please come back to me
You are so far away
This trial does not pay
I have no one
Now you have gone.

Sam Capewell (12)
The Grange School, Stourbridge

RIP

Since you have been dead
I've been staying in bed.
I miss you more each day,
As I sit and I pray.
Life isn't the same without you here,
All that's left, is pain and fear.

David Tibbetts (12)
The Grange School, Stourbridge

The Stables

As daylight dawns the horses are there,
As I take a stroll to check on my mare.
The smell of pasture overwhelms the yard,
All were sleeping, but woken up hard.

Work begins and play does cease,
Once tired horses gallop amongst the trees.
Tack is on, rugs removed,
Blacksmith arrives, horses are shoed.

Riders are free, exploring a wood,
Cantering over hills, trotting through mud.
Down bridle paths, winding lanes,
Tails flying, windswept manes.

Round the school, riding fast,
Adrenaline rush, circling past.
Three loop serpentine, figure of eight,
Lessons are over, back through the gate.

The sun starts setting, it's the end of the day,
The nets are filled with piles of hay.
Horses are out for a last minute run,
The stables are shut, the day is done.

Leigh Dooner (13)
The Grange School, Stourbridge

Even Though

Even though you're not here,
To me, you're forever, my dear.
You were always there
Whatever will I do without you?
You're mine and you're always here
In my heart.
We've never been apart.
Now you're gone
I will never forget you!

Alice Barker (12)
The Grange School, Stourbridge

Hello Me!

Hello Me, do you remember me?
We used to have so much fun but then you said that you'd moved on.
Well hiya Me, cos I don't forget; I'm still waiting and want you back.
Why don't you like me?
You used to never care, cos you liked who you were, but you were
never there.
Hey there Me, I want you back, please say you want me.
It's been a while and now every time we meet, we disagree.
Hello Me, can you hear the voices calling you?
They're saying, 'Come back down to Earth.
We swear we'll help you too.'
Well now I'm begging you Me, why won't you listen?
You're killing us both slowly, but you like to see our blood glisten.
Goodbye Me, I'll see you soon, I guess this is the end.
Now you've gone and killed us both cos you weren't society's friend.
See you Me, I'm sad to say, I'll miss you always,
But maybe now in death we'll reunite and change our ways!
I've been waiting for so long Me, I want us to be friends,
And maybe now in Heaven, we can be Me again.

Rhiannon Leonard (13)
The Grange School, Stourbridge

It's Time To Say Goodbye

He sits down, he's so still
but he didn't know when to write his will.
It hit him hard, a stone cold blow
he's a frozen statue from head to toe.
His family mourn as it's time
for he couldn't finish his rhyme.
This rapper's time is near to an end, as
his illness is final, just around the bend.
He goes to sleep for one final time
but he had no time to say goodbye.

Scott Lewis (13)
The Grange School, Stourbridge

Rhythm

A heartbeat is a rhythm
The rhythm of the world,
Of little babies' footsteps
And little boys and girls.
The rhythm of the buzzing bees,
And singing birds in trees,
Sound of traffic's car horns beeping,
And people's tapping feet.
Noises that come from happy families,
And one's in their distress.
The silence of the swaying trees,
And nature at its best.
Churches with the Funeral March,
But weddings in the days,
People searching for intimacy,
One's lonely with dismay.
People's overwhelming screaming,
For things that they enjoy,
People expressing how they feel,
Like saying, 'I love you!'
The beauty of the howling fox,
In the dark of the night,
Laughter echoes through the playground,
So everyone feels joyous.
Revving on the unsuspecting roads,
With its deadly events,
The silence of the daytime graveyard,
And the secrets of the night.
A heartbeat is a rhythm
The rhythm of the world.

Sarah Hughes (13)
The Grange School, Stourbridge

The Story Of My Life

This is my story, which I have told
I believe that you will understand it's very bold
It tells a certain narrative
Of how I am able to live

I started off as one day old
Dumped somewhere in the freezing cold
Litter spread over the floor
All I ate was an apple core

People passed without a glimpse
I even saw a dog, which had a limp
Days went by
I began to cry

Then in the breeze
A certain wanderer dropped their keys
They blew across to my very feet
I sat in disbelief on what I would have called a seat

She scooped me up and lay a sheet over me
I went to sleep very silently
Her hands were soft as silk
The next thing I saw was strangely a cup of heated milk

That was my life then
But now it's my big 10
I can't wait
I've even found a brand new mate
My mum.

Helena Moss (12)
The Grange School, Stourbridge

Pink

P ink is my favourite colour,
 I t can be florescent, bright or even pale.
N o one can say this colour is dull,
 K eep thinking pink!

Katharine Richards (13)
The Grange School, Stourbridge

The Jump

There was a single mum,
and with that single mum
there was a boyfriend,
and with that boyfriend,
there was a beating,
and with that beating
came bruises,
and with those bruises
came pain,
and with that pain
a young girl's great mind
turned into a bad mind,
and with that bad mind
came a cliff,
and with that cliff
came a jump,
and with that jump
came a suicide.
And it is so sad
that it takes a suicide
for a bad mind
to become a great mind.

Caylee Gutsell (12)
The Grange School, Stourbridge

Animals

A nimals are all around us
N ewly born in the spring
I n the fields the cows will eat
M ooing every bite they take
A wood is full of different creatures
L ots of animals in the world
S ee which ones that you can find.

Adam Josephs (12)
The Grange School, Stourbridge

Do You Really Think?

When you sip your cocoa
Or a refreshing drink,
When your belly's completely stuffed,
Do you really think?

When you're with your family
And other friends too,
Aren't there others out there
Who need friends just like you?

We need to get together
And help these ones out,
Many ones are dying,
Should we ignore their shout?

So next time you're in bed
Or sprawled across the couch,
Think of those without all this,
Don't be a selfish grouch!

Miriam Lynch (13)
The Grange School, Stourbridge

Teardrops of Sorrow

T eardrops sliding down your face,
E xtremely embarrassing,
A way of showing you're hurt,
R educing your sorrow.
D rops of pain,
R aining down off your face,
O pposite of what should be happening,
P erhaps they'll be gone one day, that would be simply the best.

Brendan Hoskins (13)
The Grange School, Stourbridge

Why Do We Eat?

Why do we eat chickens?
I really don't understand,
Chickens are safe, chickens are wicked,
Chickens should rule the land.

Why do we eat sheep,
Or lamb as we call it?
Sheep are warm, sheep are cuddly,
But then they turn evil, oh so suddenly.

Why do we eat cows?
And why do we call it beef?
Cows go moo, but should go baa,
And cows can help you go far.

Why do we eat pigs?
Think of all the mud it's been in,
Pigs go roly, pigs go poly,
And pigs should become holy.

Beth Crossfield (13)
The Grange School, Stourbridge

Untitled

Sometimes I want to spread my wings and fly away,
But you're the weight holding me down,
Maybe I'll come back and see you another day,
But when you're there my heart starts to drown.
Every day, every week,
Every year, you're making me weak.
While I'm all alone,
Not happy but sad,
All the things you've done to me,
Make me feel so bad.

Tessa Woodhams (13)
The Grange School, Stourbridge

The Chase

I'm running
running for my life
sweat dripping off me
Are they catching up?
Shouts and screams passing through me
What is happening behind?
Shall I jump the next fence
or keep running
running for my life.

All I do is run
I can't give in
I can't stop
People watching me as I go by
I daren't turn my head
I fear too much
I turn around the corner
to find I am surrounded
I need to think
I need to think to keep my life.

Jonathan Billington (12)
The Grange School, Stourbridge

Charity

C hoose to help people in need,
H elp families to learn, live and feed.
A gony can stop with just one pound,
R esearch, so the cure can be found.
 I n Africa every three seconds a child dies,
T his is thanks to politics' lies,
Y ou can help save lots of lives.

Melissa Clements (13)
The Grange School, Stourbridge

A Recipe For Trouble

You will need:
Two brothers and sisters
a big prize
and a small room.

Method:
Mix two brothers and sisters
in a small room.
Add the big prize.
Leave to set for 5 mins.
Open the door.

Expert's tip:
The bigger the prize,
the better the result.

Julien Bigot (13)
The Grange School, Stourbridge

Mates

M aking you laugh and smile
A lways around, ready to listen
T elling secrets, sharing memories
E ither old friends or new
S pecial too and forever.

Hannah Quance (13)
The Grange School, Stourbridge

Food

F rom a bowl to the hole,
O h, why don't they shove it in with a funnel?
O ranges mashed up travels on the train,
D ad thinks my mouth is a tunnel.

Katie Shaw (12)
The Grange School, Stourbridge

Not All People Have Great Minds

I sit in a corner like I always do
Facing the wall like my parents want me to

I curl on the floor, hurt from another beating
Ready to hide my bruises, I go to bed without eating

My brother always got my parents' attention
While I was at school for another detention

I've struggled through life and made it this far
But then my dad got hit by a car

It wasn't my fault, though I got the blame,
She didn't care, to her it's the same

They wouldn't believe me, I'm just dirt on the floor
Should be kicked and shut behind a locked door

Maybe soon people will see
I was a good kid from a bad family

Every night I held the gun to my head
I'll never do it they all said

A child later that night was found dead
A suicide? Ill-treated some said.

Lauren Seex (11)
The Grange School, Stourbridge

Silent Squirrel

So quiet, you could hear a buzzing bee,
When a squirrel moves swiftly but silently,
From tree to tree,
He moves gracefully,
Be careful you don't scare him,
He might just flee,
Unless you tiptoe really quietly.

Danielle Staples (12)
The Grange School, Stourbridge

Open Road

Life is like the open road
Darting around in neon light
Caught in an endless stream of traffic
All trying to make their way.

The road trails behind you endlessly
You can only see as far as your headlights shine
Thin beams of yellow rays
And somehow you make the whole journey that way.

The road is getting rocky now
Your tyres are getting weary
You're so near to your destination
And then you crash.

Engulfed in your own headlights
So close to point B
But what you don't know is you've already reached it
Back at the start again.

Life is like the open road.

Jemma Hayfield-Husbands (12)
The Grange School, Stourbridge

Great Minds

The wind crashes off the bonnet
Pistons pumping
Engine roaring
Suspension bombing.

The spoiler keeps me on the ground
Rims spinning
Brakes clutching
My driver's winning.

James Griffiths (12)
The Grange School, Stourbridge

The Creature

Like a high speed performance car it ruthlessly goes,
Well hidden it prefers.
It scares people malevolently, perplexing them at what it is doing,
The animal kingdom, especially the rainforest,
Experiences this every day,
Scaring people it likes.

But as he grows a bit more he comes out of the dark
And stops being shy,
He slides about without a thought for what he's doing,
Terrifying people he still enjoys,
But a drastic, fatal 'accident' kills him,
Scaring people he likes.

His family in 'bits' and tears,
Emotions running wild,
He did like to scare people, he did like to slide around,
But his life had to end quick,
He didn't get to see the mysteries of the world,
Scaring people he did like.

Thomas Wilkins (12)
The Grange School, Stourbridge

Great Minds

They are quiet and old
Bossed about, do as they're told

Sit in the corner, neglected
Taken for granted, not respected

They're sad and being used
Beaten, bruised, day after day being abused

It's a shame because they're kind
And there is a ton load of knowledge in their mind.

Rebecca Savoy (12)
The Grange School, Stourbridge

Bullied

Where's my bag?
Up in the air,
I ran to fetch it,
They stare and glare.

I'm hungry today,
Where's my money?
They have stolen it again,
They think it's funny.

They have kicked me twice now,
It really hurts,
They have torn all my clothes,
I've got 16 shirts.

My mum doesn't know,
She never will,
I'm at the hospital now,
Because I'm really ill.

Alexia Smith (12)
The Grange School, Stourbridge

Me, Myself And I

Sometimes I need to think about me,
Myself,
And I,
What time is it? Who am I with?
Sometimes myself is all I have,
My friends go after the latest craze,
But I don't want to be a sheep,
So maybe I want to fit in,
But all I need is
     Me, myself and I.

Emma Fisher (11)
The Grange School, Stourbridge

Friends

Friends are forever,
Friends are great,
Friends give you an alibi,
When you're out late,
Friends are always on your side,
But not when you have lied.

Hannah Mitchinson (11)
The Grange School, Stourbridge

Opposite Poem

As soft as the fur of a purring cat,
As hard as an iron horseshoe.

As wet as the roaring sea,
As dry as a dog's bone.

As fast as the cheating cheetah,
As slow as a sleeping tortoise.

As short as the seven dwarves,
As long as a piece of string.

As sweet as a packet of wine gums,
As sour as a fresh lemon.

As round as a new football,
As square as building blocks.

As silly as a children's clown,
As cunning as an old fox.

As hot as a burning fire,
As cold as frozen ice.

As loud as a birthday party,
As quiet as a house mouse.

Stacey Vernon (14)
The Orchard Centre, Wolverhampton

Opposite Poem

As soft as a purring cat
As hard as a steel baseball bat
As wet as a slimy fish
As dry as the desert sand
As fast as a hunting cheetah
As slow as a slimy snail
As short as a needle on a speedo
As long as an axle under a car
As sweet as a spoonful of sugar
As sour as a Eye Popper sweet
As round as a brand new football
As square as a face on a Rubix cube
As cunning as a prowling fox
As hot as the burning sun
As cold as a frozen ice cube.

Maverick Marshall (13)
The Orchard Centre, Wolverhampton

Katy Hubbard's Spell

(Inspired by Shakespeare's 'Macbeth')

Double, double, toil and trouble
Fire burn and cauldron bubble
Round about the cauldron go
In a teacher's bogey throw
A rotten school dinner thick with mould
A dead head teacher stiff and cold.

Double, double, toil and trouble
Fire burn and cauldron bubble
A pinch of oozing squeezed pimple
Make it vile yet keep it simple
Granny's teeth mixed with hog's blood
Then the charm is foul and good.

Katy Hubbard (13)
The Orchard Centre, Wolverhampton

Jordan's Chant

(Inspired by Shakespeare's 'Macbeth')

Double double, toil and trouble
Fire burn and cauldron bubble
Round about the cauldron go
In a mouldy turkey throw
A hamster's body, stiff and cold
Like a sausage roll thick with mould
A greedy man-eating snake
A prickly nettle dug up in the dark
Head of car and stomach of frog
Wings of bats and tail of dog
Cool it with a snake's blood
Then the charm is firm and good.

Jordan Moulton (14)
The Orchard Centre, Wolverhampton

Natalie's Double Trouble

(Inspired by Shakespeare's 'Macbeth')

Double, double
Bubble, bubble
Trouble, trouble
Round about the cauldron go
In a teacher's dentures throw
A rotten apple thick with mould
A sewer rat's body stiff and cold
Sparkling diamond rings
A baby owl's wing
Tail of grass snake
In the cauldron boil and bake
Head of cat and toe of rat
Cool it with a snake's blood
Then the charm is fine and good.

Natalie Richards (14)
The Orchard Centre, Wolverhampton

Stephanie's Spell

(Inspired by Shakespeare's 'Macbeth')

Double, double, toil and trouble
Fire burn, cauldron bubble

Stir and stir the cauldron go
Dirty fingernails in they throw

Crawling and creepy spider legs
Stir it with an elephant's toe

Black skin of cockroaches
Munch and crunch for lunch

The snake's slimy blood
Goes round and round

Steam and smoke as they cough
As it looks like mouldy Scotch broth

Double, double, toil and trouble
Fire burn and cauldron bubble.

Stephanie Gard (14)
The Orchard Centre, Wolverhampton

Ten Things Found In A Witch's Bag

(Based on 'Ten Things Found In A Wizard's Pocket' by Ian McMillan)

A black cat with ginger spots,
A broom made out of sticks,
A wand that turns people into goats,
Multicoloured lipstick and nail varnish,
Toenails from dead people,
Potion to give you spots,
A purple wig with blood on it,
Bloodshot eyeballs,
3 giggling witches,
A pair of bright green socks.

Laura Whitehouse (13)
The Orchard Centre, Wolverhampton

Danny's Opposite Poem

As soft as a cotton wool ball,
as hard as a cast iron bench.
As wet as the Atlantic Ocean,
as dry as the desert on a real hot day.
As fast as a cheetah after his prey,
as slow as a tortoise trying to run away.
As short as a sharp sewing needle,
as long as a winding Amazon jungle river.
As sweet as a rich chocolate pudding,
as sour as freshly squeezed lemon juice.
As round as car alloy wheels,
as square as a Rubix cube face.
As silly as a clown on a unicycle,
as cunning as a fox after a rabbit.
As hot as the Sahara desert on a scorching hot day,
as cold as Antarctica.
As loud as a big car exhaust,
as quiet as the country fields on a warm summer's day.

Danny Walker (14)
The Orchard Centre, Wolverhampton

I Like, I Hate

(Based on 'I Like, I Hate' by Louise Stewart)

I like the smell of strawberries being cut in half with a spoon
I hate the smell of cheese that has been left in the fridge for weeks
I like the sound of rustling leaves because it makes me feel good
I hate the sound of an old blackboard that's been used day after day
I like the sight of a bonfire flickering into the dark sky
I hate the sight of people fighting in the war in Iraq
I like the taste of oranges squirting into my mouth
I hate the taste of marmalade which has long bits of dry oranges in
I like the feel of an egg that is unbroken
I hate the feel of bubblegum under the table at school.

David Whitehouse (13)
The Orchard Centre, Wolverhampton

I Like, I Hate

(Based on 'I Like, I Hate' by Lousie Stewart)

I like the smell of petrol at the petrol station,
I hate the smell of poo in the toilet.

I like to hear the crunching frost on the grass,
I hate to hear the squeaking on the white board.

I like the taste of Galaxy chocolate,
I hate the taste of fish from the fish and chip shop.

I like the touch of the water from a swimming pool,
I hate the touch of polystyrene plates and cups.

I like the sight of the full moon at night,
I hate the sight of sick down the toilet and the corridors.

Scott Miles (11)
The Orchard Centre, Wolverhampton

I Like, I Hate

(Based on 'I Like, I Hate' by Louise Stewart)

I like the smell of juicy, round oranges that have just been peeled,
I hate the smell of mouldy green cheese that has been in the fridge
for weeks.
I like the sound of a girl's sweet voice,
I hate the sound of a toilet flushing.
I like the sweet taste of melted chocolate that has just touched
your tongue,
I hate the taste of fish with a hard coat of batter.
I like the feel of a soft blanket that has just touched your skin,
I hate the feel of an egg that has just been broken in your hand.
I like the sight of the sunset going down after a long day,
I hate the sight of a dirty nose that has not been cleaned in days.

Joshua Williams (11)
The Orchard Centre, Wolverhampton

Spider's Web

Glistening, glittering on a garden gate.
Dewdrops dangling like diamonds on a silver thread.
The web floats, fragile, fine and free.
An intricate lacy, pearly-white creation.
The spider suspended on her bejewelled masterpiece.
Watchful, waiting and wondering.
Drifting, quivering, a queen on her silken silvery throne.
She is an artist and sculptor entangled into one.
Glistening, glittering on a golden gate.

Ellie Freer (12)
Walton High School, Stafford

Black

Black are the deathly demons unseen
Black are the shadows in the deep, dark forest
Black is the night sky with the sparkling silver stars
Black are the unknown eyes watching your every move
Black is the colour of the jet black jewel against your pale white skin
Black is the horror of the unliving, rising from the dead
The end of the world is *black,* no one can see it, no one can hear it.

Rebecca England (11)
Walton High School, Stafford

My Dog Ruby!

R uby is my doggie, my bestest friend too,
U can always rely on Ruby and she'll be there for you.
B ut she is also naughty, a mucky pup too, her favourite games
  are chewing sticks and eating horse poo.
Y et I will always love her, and yes it really is true, if you're ever sad
  or glum, she'll lick and comfort you.

Robyn Goodfellow (12)
Walton High School, Stafford

How Do You Feel?

How do you feel?
Angry? Depressed?
Maybe you're lonely,
Or feeling quite stressed?
Do you want someone to talk to,
Or to just be alone?
Do you feel you're unsettled
At school and at home?
Do you feel miserable or cheery,
Or perhaps you're both?
Are you crying one moment
And the next you're aglow?
Do you feel proud
To be who you are,
Or are others around you
Making life rather hard?
Do you hold up your head
And laugh with the crowd,
Or sulk in the corner
With your head bowed?
Do you wish to be happy,
Do you like to be glad,
Or do you prefer to be lonely,
Sorrowful and sad?
Well, to feel all of these feelings,
As hard as it seems,
Is only human
Unfortunately.

Hayley Chatfield (12)
Walton High School, Stafford

Autumn

Crisp leaves snapping underfoot
Foraging squirrel darting, looking for a nut
Sparks crackling from the bonfire
The cold easterly wind frosting the cow mire
The frosty moonlight hitting like a dart
But the firework celebrations warming the heart
Roasted marshmallows dripping on the floor
These are the things that autumn is for.

Alex Shaw (11)
Walton High School, Stafford

Friends Always

Friends bring joy, friends bring smiles
Friends bring laughter all the while
Friends share secrets, friends share love
A friendship will last to the stars above
Friends make you happy when they are around
They don't tell your secrets, they keep them safe and sound.

Sarah Daniels (12)
Walton High School, Stafford

Christmas Tree

In a little window stands a tinselled Christmas tree,
bright with colours red and gold, a lovely thing to see.
Lighting up the dingy street for every passer-by,
With a glow that lifts the spirit and delights the dull brown eye.

Amy Courtney (12)
Walton High School, Stafford

Pirate Ship

Whoosh! Whoosh! The waves were rolling.

On the captain's shoulder sat a parrot, so green,
On his head was an eye patch and some scars, they looked mean.

Whoosh! Whoosh! The waves were rolling.

'Attack!' cried a voice from above the huge mast,
So the cannonballs fired with a terrible blast.

Whoosh! Whoosh! The waves were rolling.

On the front of the boat was a hideous head,
It looked like a sailor that had been shot dead.

Whoosh! Whoosh! The waves were rolling.

The pirate flag flew high in the air,
Then the boy woke up, what a scary nightmare.

Whoosh! Whoosh! The waves were rolling.

Jim Mulherin (12)
Walton High School, Stafford

Sunset Beach In Tenerife

Swinging palm trees blowing gently in the breeze
The blazing sun scorching your back
Cool hotel called Sunset Beach
The grey, mysterious mist around Mount Tidy
Ice-cold ice cream melting in the blazing sun
Creamy cocktails with cherries on colourful umbrellas
Turquoise blue water shimmering in the moonlight
Noise, activity
People having fun
Karaoke, scuba diving
Something for everyone.

Jasmin Hellard (12)
Walton High School, Stafford

Tiger

The velvet tigers in the jungle
Prowl and pounce with powerful jaws
Camouflage shaggy fur
Padded paws dancing
A wet, soft nose and whiskers a-standing
Evil, gleaming, glistening eyes
Pearly, piercing, sharp white teeth
A mane of fine fur and a hidden sleek body
With whiskers as long as bulrushes
And stripes of black and white
All different shapes and patterns
Bashing against long winding tall grass
All the beautiful shades of graceful green
The velvet tigers in the jungle
Prowl and pounce with powerful jaws.

Emma Child (11)
Walton High School, Stafford

Art

Many talents, many skills,
Drawing people, or trees and hills.

This arty world is full of delight,
Artists work by day, by night.

Animals and creatures people draw,
Still life, portraits, collage and more.

Paint just splattered on the page,
Paintings of herbs, like thyme and sage.

Different drawings of mystical things,
Like fairies with sparkling wings.

From beaches to mountains,
People to fountains.

Think about it, what do you draw?

Lucy Thompson (11)
Walton High School, Stafford

Love

You can never see it,
But it's always there,
Whether you are young or old,
Every moment you should
Treasure it.

The richest jewel of all,
That everyone can have,
Hurried hearts beat for it,
Romance, roses, chocolates and more,
Treasure it.

Red is the colour that symbolises it,
It is special,
But there is a flaw,
You will always end up hurt,
So love,
Treasure it.

Hannah Fyfe (12)
Walton High School, Stafford

Detention!

The teachers are shouting,
'Detention, detention!'
In French they are shouting,
'Retenue, retenue!'
In English they are shouting,
'Detention!' by Charles Dickens.
In history they are shouting,
'Detention!' by Henry VIII.
At lunch they're shouting,
'Sit here, not there!'
And school council is begging,
The school to change its staff.

Mike Green (11)
Walton High School, Stafford

Young Writers - Great Minds - Inspirations From The Midlands

Tsunami

The winds circled us
Growling and whining
Small children began panicking and crying.

Bang! The Earth shuddered
Moving houses and shops
People startled by sudden shocks.

The sea groaned and frothed on top
The sky turned dark black
And people ran home by different tracks.

Waves churned and rose high above
Before crashing down
Upon different towns.

Houses fell down
People died
Lots and lots of children cried.

Amy-May Boyce (12)
Walton High School, Stafford

Green

Green is . . .
The colour of envy
Mouldy cheese
Mould
Jealousy
Emerald gems
Leaves in the summer
The colour of you when you are feeling ill
The blanket of green in your garden.

Katrina Tompkins (11)
Walton High School, Stafford

Chickens

They're clucking
They're pecking
They're flapping but they can't fly
But when they're taken away from farms
They go to supermarkets
Then you might go and buy them
Or maybe someone else will
But if you take it home
Have a good Sunday lunch.

Mikey Pointon (11)
Walton High School, Stafford

Start Of The End

Start of the beginning, the start of a race
Race - where everyone wants to win
Win - nowhere near to losing
Losing - but wanting to carry on
On with a flick of a switch
Switch - to light up the world
World - let's don't let it end
End . .. of this poem.

Sam Coates (12)
Walton High School, Stafford

Friendship

Friendship is like a long daisy chain
That lasts forever and ever.
Friendship is a happy feeling,
Hopefully you won't break up, ever.
You will never see it no matter how hard you try,
You have to trust it's there,
You'll do anything for friends,
Because you really care.

Megan Hitchin (12)
Walton High School, Stafford

Red

Rubies
Shining in the jeweller's window
Shining all day and night

Blood
Coming from a cut in my leg
Hurting as it bleeds, oww!

Walls
In my bedroom
Darkening in on me

Walton ties
To make us look smart
But we're just ordinary kids

Lipstick
Covering girls' lips
Leaves in the autumn.

Lucinda Grinsted (11)
Walton High School, Stafford

Winter

I wake up in the morning freezing cold
The fields are patterned like ice
All the trees are frozen
The water has a layer of ice.

A thick mist hangs above
You can't see very far
Everyone is still in bed
And the engine's frozen in the car.

The moon and sun still in the sky
School is closed and the road is blocked
Snow is piled on the house
We can't get out, the door is locked.

Ben Thompson (11)
Walton High School, Stafford

Best Friends

Last night I dreamt
Of Ahmed and Mohammed
And their solemn faces,
Guiding me through the darkness
Of Gaza by night.
Gunfire flickered beneath my eyelids
And tanks groaned their way past my sleeping face,
And still I am stunned by the boy's sheer,
Unquestioning trust, a trust I could never equal,
Myself being both too old already and too sheltered.
In this sleep I have known nothing
Till waking, when I was shaken so violently
That in a flash, a momentarily lifting of ignorance,
I saw:
    Processions calling praise for the martyrs;
    Printed smiles proudly plastering the town's walls,
    Closed in and oppressive in the heat;
    Anger and resentment rises like raging hot air in the school room.
    The boys are being taught to be soldiers -
    To throw stones, grenades, lives away -
    For the war they have lived all their lives in, but don't understand.

Mohammed says that he worries he shall lose Ahmed.
He says that if Ahmed is to be martyred he should want to die too.
He consoles his mother, tells her she would have three other children
Still to care for.
Mohammed is just a little boy, and he is full of someone else's anger.

A shell has landed.
Shrapnel scatters.
And I wake with the white light and ringing filling my head.

Holly Corfield-Carr (17)
Walton High School, Stafford

Darkness

The night is near,
Street lights flickering on slowly,
People going to bed,
Dreams,
Bad dreams,
Car lights reflecting from windows,
Foxes slowly creeping in gardens,
Hedgehogs coming out of their nests,
Scuttering across roads, dodging cars,
Owls swooping out of their trees catching their tea,
Darkness is here.

Jack Cuthbert (12)
Walton High School, Stafford

Tsunami

The sun blazed down on the scorched sand where I lay,
My mind drifting in thoughts far away,
And then it came that unstoppable wave,
I managed to duck into a cave,
The water swept me out and into the street,
Then I felt a tug on my feet,
A child was there holding on for her life,
Her face was wrinkled and full of strife,
She disappeared into the blue abyss,
Evermore to be missed . . .

Brad Giffard (13)
Wigmore High School, Wigmore

A Soldier's Belief - A War Poem

(Inspired by 'Suicide In The Trenches' by Siegfried Sassoon)

My dear children I will soon be back,
But this is my call of duty.
To win this war, to fight for my country,
To wear a British uniform.

I am leaving now, I am going to fight,
But when I arrive I will not die.
I will think of you,
My children and my wife.
I will not let those Germans
Take my life.

I am confident, I have belief,
I will not think of death or defeat.
I arrive at the trenches, it's worse than it sounds,
Soldiers dying everywhere, falling to the ground.

It's the moment the soldiers dread,
They waited for the call,
Go, go over the top,
The head soldier did ball.

They run, they head for the trench,
Praying and hoping for their life,
Thinking, wondering, screaming,
Is this the end of the fight?

I'm lying in the trenches,
I feel rotten to the bone.
But I died for my country,
That country is my own.

Laura Bradley-Smith (13)
Windsor Park CE Middle School, Uttoxeter

War To The Grave

(Inspired by poetry of the First World War)

Too young to go to war,
But I'm going all the same.
Just think, I'll be a hero,
When I come back again.

Marching to the harbour,
Uniformed, ready to go,
Someone standing in the crowd,
Wailing and crying, 'What do they know?'

Arrived at the trenches,
It's different to how I thought,
Devastation and destruction,
Another soldier caught.

Too terrified to speak,
Bombs and gunning all around,
All I feel inside is nausea,
People falling to the ground.

Trench foot setting in now,
I feel rotten to the core,
Feels like an eternal battle,
I just can't take it anymore.

The sights and sounds of war,
Will be taken to my grave,
No one will ever know,
The bravery we gave.

Jennifer Lee-Bromley (13)
Windsor Park CE Middle School, Uttoxeter

My Daddy Has Gone Somewhere

(Inspired by poetry of the First World War)

My daddy has gone somewhere
My mummy is crying again
Second time this week I say
I am sure something's wrong

I see him! I see him again!
He waves, he waves to me again
Then as quickly as he came, he vanished
At night I see flashes
Flashes in the distance
Gunshots and bangs
I can never get to sleep
My daddy has gone somewhere.

2 years and still no sight
Sometimes I feel such guilt
Sometimes I feel scared.

I see him! I see him in the street!
But when I run he vanishes again
My daddy has gone somewhere.

Sometimes I say to myself
'Daddy, please come back?'
I miss you, I miss you
Why did you go?
Why, why, oh why?

David Harris (12)
Windsor Park CE Middle School, Uttoxeter

Attack, Attack

(Inspired by 'Suicide In The Trenches' by Siegfried Sassoon)

Attack, attack,
Gunshots going,
Deafening my ears.

Attack, attack,
I was confident,
Until I came out here.

Attack, attack,
Some gas has come,
I hear choking everywhere.

Attack, attack,
The air's all green,
Nothing can be seen.

Attack, attack,
The gas has gone,
The dead are all around.

Attack, attack,
I knew that man,
Now lying dead down there.

Attack, attack,
I've just been shot,
I'm lying down in pain,
I am now dead for my country.

Sarah Lomas (12)
Windsor Park CE Middle School, Uttoxeter

Bang! Bang!

(Inspired by poetry of Rupert Brooke)

I'm sitting here thinking of my child and wife,
Will I return home to continue my life?
Holding my gun through the mist and the cold,
'Kill them, kill them!' so I am told.

But they're just people like me and you,
It isn't fair, they've a family too.
I must survive day and night,
I shouldn't have to put up with this fearful fight.

I watch men die in front of me,
It's horrific what I see.
Before I saw what I saw,
I was proud that I was going to fight in the war.

Now all I feel is pure dread,
Nearly all the men are dead.
The Germans have come now, I must leave you,
But I want you to know that I'll always love our child and you too.

Georgette Storey (13)
Windsor Park CE Middle School, Uttoxeter

Gas - Gas - Gas!

(Inspired by 'Dulce Est Decorum Est' by Wilfred Owen)

Gas, gas, gas everywhere,
'Come on,' said the corporal, 'don't stand and stare.'
That's all we ever hear nowadays,
'Cause that's all the corporal ever bloomin' says.
Living in the trenches ain't so bloomin' good,
All we ever do is walk over soggy mud.

Wish I could see my wife and son,
But all I ever do is fire my bloomin' gun,
Killing all the Nazis ain't so bloomin' fun,
All we ever do is shoot, shoot, shoot!
Half of us don't wear any boots,
I don't want to kill the Germans,
I'm sure they don't want to kill us too,
But because of the stupid government,
That's what we have to do.
I want to go home to see my wife,
So I can improve on our kid's life.

Michael Gascoigne (13)
Windsor Park CE Middle School, Uttoxeter

War Poem

(Inspired by 'Soldier' by Rupert Brooke)

Here I come brave and prepared,
Aware that I could die,
In my uniform no fear at all,
We could win, we could lose,
Got my gun, hear me shoot,
But now I'm changing in my mind.

Sounds like thunder, sounds like dread,
Sweating, shaking, under pressure,
Let me out, let me out,
Terrified like a mouse smelling death and seeing death,
Missing home, getting diseases,
Walking through the boggy mud in the trenches.

I was brave, I had no fear,
But now I think that I'll be dead in no-man's-land,
Shelter, shelter, gas masks on,
The green light sea we're swamping through.

I had no fear, I feel no guilt,
Never had such bad nausea,
Such devastation, such devastation,
War should never have happened,
People, friends and family dying,
So now mine's gone, I'm all alone.

Lauren Swinson (13)
Windsor Park CE Middle School, Uttoxeter

Everlasting Fight

(Inspired by 'Suicide In The Trenches' by Siegfried Sassoon)

Before I went to the dreadful hell,
I loved my life, I taught my kids to spell,
And then the day came when I had to leave,
Knowing for them I would grieve,
I cried and cried till I could no more,
No more for my body was extremely sore,
When I put on my uniform,
The enemy I had to deform,
Living in the trenches, living in the trenches,
Soldiers rotting made even us stench,
Trench foot,
An infected cut,
Poisoned blood,
And up to your neck in thick black mud.
If this is a sign of winning the fight,
Then perhaps the government should have a look at the sight,
Screaming, whining, that's all I can hear,
The only chance of winning is to drown myself in beer,
Then a shell dropped right in front of me,
The chance of surviving is one to one hundred and three,
Now I'm in Heaven,
I've met a German,
He's just like you and me!
I don't see the point of this fight,
Now I must go to an everlasting night,
Because I fought in the everlasting fight.

Lydia Nadine (12)
Windsor Park CE Middle School, Uttoxeter

Perhaps, Perhaps

(Inspired by the poetry of Vera Britain)

Perhaps, perhaps
He'll be back one day,
In his smart uniform,
I fear the worst,
I think the best.

Perhaps, perhaps
He'll be back one day,
The nervous, worried, anxious man
Shaking, shouting, nausea occurs
In the boggy, muddy trench.

Perhaps, perhaps
He'll be back one day,
The sweet, kind, generous husband,
I am upset and want him back.

Perhaps, perhaps
He'll be back one day,
They might end the war today.

I knew he'd be back this day,
The kids so happy when he returned,
Their dad's back and we are all so glad.

Stephanie Gear (12)
Windsor Park CE Middle School, Uttoxeter